CW01659091

J. B. Bury

The History of Barbarians

OK Publishing 2021

J. B. Bury

The History of Barbarians

The Invasion of Europe by the Barbarians

Published by
MUSAICUM
Books

- Advanced Digital Solutions & High-Quality book Formatting -

musaicumbooks@okpublishing.info

2021 OK Publishing

ISBN 978-80-272-7296-9

Contents

Lecture 1: The Germans and Their Wanderings 11

Lecture 2: The Roman Empire and the Germans 19

Lecture 3: The Clash of Roman and Barbarian 26

Lecture 4: The Visigothic Entry into the Empire 35

Lecture 5: The Raiding of Italy and Gaul 44

Lecture 6: The Visigoths in Italy and Gaul 52

Lecture 7: Gaul, Spain, and Africa in Transition 61

Lecture 8: A New Menace to the Empire 70

Lecture 9: Attila's Attack on Gaul and Italy 76

Lecture 10: Decline of the Roman Power in the West 85

Lecture 11: The Ostrogothic Conquest of Italy 93

Lecture 12: Visigoths and Franks in Gaul 108

Lecture 13: The Reign of Clovis 116

Lecture 14: The Lombard Invasion of Italy 128

Lecture 15: The Lombard Law 137

Lecture 1:
The Germans and Their Wanderings

EARLY GERMAN HISTORY – WEST GERMANS AND EAST GERMANS – POLITICAL INSTITUTIONS OF THE GERMANS – EARLY GOTHIC MIGRATIONS

EARLY GERMAN HISTORY

The present series of lectures is designed to give a broad and general view of the long sequence of the migratory movements of the northern barbarians which began in the third and fourth centuries A.D. and cannot be said to have terminated till the ninth. This long process shaped Europe into its present form, and it must be grasped in its broad outlines in order to understand the framework of modern Europe.

There are two ways in which the subject may be treated, two points of view from which the sequence of changes which broke up the Roman Empire may be regarded. We may look at the process, in the earliest and most important stage, from the point of view of the Empire which was being dismembered or from that of the barbarians who were dismembering it. We may stand in Rome and watch the strangers sweeping over her provinces; or we may stand east of the Rhine and north of the Danube, amid the forests of Germany, and follow the fortunes of the men who issued thence, winning new habitations and entering on a new life. Both methods have been followed by modern writers. Gibbon and many others have told the story from the side of the Roman Empire, but all the principal barbarian peoples – not only those who founded permanent states, but even those who formed only transient kingdoms – have had each its special historian. One naturally falls into the habit of contemplating these events from the Roman side because the early part of the story has come down to us in records which were written from the Roman side. We must, however, try to see things from both points of view.

The barbarians who dismembered the Empire were mainly Germans. It is not till the sixth century that people of another race – the Slavs – appear upon the scene. Those who approach for the first time the study of the beginnings of medieval history will probably find it difficult to group and locate clearly in their minds the multitude of Germanic peoples who surge over the scene in distracting confusion. The apparent confusion vanishes, of course, with familiarity, and the movements fall into a certain order. But at the very outset the study of the period may be simplified by drawing a line of division within the Germanic world. This capital line of division is geographical, but it has its basis in historical facts. It is the distinction of the West Germans from the East Germans. To understand this division we must go back for a moment into the early history of the Germans.

WEST GERMANS AND EAST GERMANS

In the second millennium B.C. the homes of the Germanic peoples were in southern Scandinavia, in Denmark, and in the adjacent lands between the Elbe and the Oder. East of them beyond the Oder were Baltic or Lettic peoples, who are now represented by Lithuanians and Letts. The lands west of the Elbe, to the Rhine, were occupied by Celts.

After 1000 B.C. a double movement of expansion began. The Germans between the Oder and the Elbe pressed westward, displacing the Celts. The boundary between the Celts and Germans advanced to the west, and by about 200 B.C. it had been pushed forward to the Rhine, and southward to the Main. Throughout this period the Germans had been also pressing up the Elbe. Soon after 100 B.C. southern Germany had been occupied, and they were attempting to flood Gaul. This inundation was stemmed by Julius Caesar. Now all these peoples who expanded over western Germany from their original seats between Oder and Elbe we will class as the West Germans.

The other movement was a migration from Scandinavia to the opposite coasts of the Baltic, between the Oder and the Vistula, and ultimately beyond the Vistula. This migration seems to have taken place at a later period than the beginning of the expansion of the West Germans. It is placed by a recent authority, Kossinna, in the later bronze period, between 600 and 300 B.C. By the latter date they seem to have pressed right up to the Vistula to the neighbourhood of the Carpathians. These comers from Scandinavia formed a group which in dialect and customs may be distinguished from the West Germans, as well as in their geographical position; and we designate them as East Germans. The distinction is convenient because the historical roles of these two divisions of the German race were different. There is also a third division, the *North Germans* of Scandinavia; but with them we are not concerned.

In the period with which we have to do, the West Germans are comparatively settled geographically, whereas the East Germans are migratory. Now it is not difficult to understand why this is so. All the ancient Germans were shepherds and hunters. They had some agriculture before the time of Julius Caesar, but not much. Central Europe till well into the Middle Ages consisted largely of dense forests and marshlands. There were, however, districts free from wood, and the absence of wood was the circumstance which largely determined the early settlements of the Germans. Geographers are able to fix the position of such tracts of steppe land by means of the remains of steppe plants – plants which cannot live either in the forest or on cultivated soil – and also by the remains of animals which are characteristic of the steppe. Cases of such land, for instance, are the plain of the upper Rhine and the eastern portion of the Harz district.

When a people settled down in such a district they could live, as a rule peaceably and contentedly, on their flocks and herds, until their number began to increase considerably. Then their pasture land, limited by the surrounding forests, became insufficient, and presently the food question grew pressing. There were three solutions open: they might take to agriculture, which would enable them to support a far larger population in the same area; they might extend their pasturage by clearing the forest; or they might reduce their superfluity of population by emigrating. The third resource was that which they regularly adopted; the other two were opposed to their nature and instincts. A portion would emigrate and seize a new habitation elsewhere. This, of course, meant war and conquest. This process went on at the expense of the Celts until Central Europe became entirely Germanised. They would then have naturally advanced westward or southward, but the Roman power hindered them. Thus the Western Germans, having no further room for expansion, shut in on the east by their own kinsfolk who were tightly packed, on the west and south by the Roman Empire, were forced to find another solution for the food question. Perforce they took to tilling the land. We have direct evidence for this important change in their habits. Caesar describes the Germans as mainly a pastoral people: they did practise agriculture, but it was little. About one hundred and fifty years later Tacitus describes them as practising agriculture. This transformation, then, from a preeminently pastoral state to an agricultural state came about during the century after their geographical expansion was arrested by the power of Rome. That period was a critical stage in their development. Now remember that all this applies to the West Germans: it is the West Germans to whom the descriptions of Caesar and Tacitus relate. The East Germans beyond the Elbe were by no means in the same position. They were not hemmed in in the same way. Their neighbours to the east and south were barbarians – Slavs and others – who did not hinder their freedom of movement, and so there was no motive to give up their pastoral and migratory habits.

You can now understand how in the second century A.D. the East and West Germans are distinguished not only by geographical position but also by the different stages of civilisation which they have reached. The West Germans are agricultural and have attained those relatively settled habits which agriculture induces. The East Germans are chiefly pastoral and represent a stage from which the West Germans began to emerge a couple of centuries before.

I may illustrate this further by referring to a different interpretation of the evidence which was put forward by Dr. Felix Dahn, who devoted his life and numerous works to early German history. He starts from the great change from the unsettled life of the Germans in the time of Caesar, when they depended chiefly on pasture and the chase, to the relatively settled life, in which agriculture predominated, corresponding to the description of Tacitus. Using this fact as a minor premise, he lays down as a general rule that when such a change takes place from an unsettled to a settled life increase in population is a natural consequence. And from these two premises he argues that Germany increased largely in population. Such an increase, he says, would only begin to tell four or five generations after a people had adopted settled habits; that means 120 or 150 years. If we take about A.D. 20-30 as the middle point of the period of change – between Caesar and Tacitus – then four or five generations bring us down to the period A.D. 140-180, just the time in which the East German migratory movement began. He concludes that increase of population, due to the change from pastoral to agricultural habits, was the cause of the migrations and the expansive movements which began in the second century A.D.

You will readily perceive the fallacy which underlies this interesting argument. Dr. Dahn applies to the Germans as a whole, and to the East Germans in particular, the evidence of Tacitus, which is true only of the West Germans, who came under Roman observation. The picture of Tacitus is taken entirely from the West Germans; of the German peoples beyond the Elbe the Romans knew little more than the names and geographical positions of some of them. Thus Dr. Dahn does not take us any further. Increase of population, which means the food question, was the driving force in the whole process of German expansion from prehistoric times onward, and it was the main cause, no doubt, of the movement which began in the second century A.D.; but the new agricultural habits of the West Germans had nothing to do with it.

Before dealing with this movement, which is a movement of East Germans, I have a word more to say about the West Germans. The old names of the West German peoples between the Rhine and Elbe are preserved by Tacitus and in other records of early imperial history. But in the later times with which we have to do now, these names have almost entirely disappeared. We have no longer to do with the Tencteri, the Cherusci, the Chatti, etc.; we have to do with the Alamanni, the Franks, the Saxons, the Thuringians. The reason of this change is that from the end of the second century western Germany had been re-formed by a process of federation and blending of groups of smaller peoples in large unities. Thus the *Alamanni* were a composite nation formed from the Suevian tribes, and others, on the upper Rhine. In the same way the peoples on the lower Rhine had formed a loose conglomerate under the name of *Franks*. This name Frank or 'free' seems to have been given as a distinction from the neighbouring peoples who were subject to Rome in the province of Lower Germany. Between the Weser and Elbe, and inland to the Harz mountains, another group of people was collected under the name of *Saxons*. The tribes who gave the name to the whole confederation had come from beyond the mouth of the Elbe, near the neck of the Cimbric peninsula; for our purpose they are West Germans. But among the West Germans they were exceptional in the length of their migrations.

The Saxons were parted from the Franks by the intervening *Frisians*; and south of the Saxons were the Thuringians who mainly represented the ancient Hermunduri.

It has been sometimes questioned whether these groups were really confederates, bound by a definite league. The fact seems proved by a text of Ammianus Marcellinus who, in speaking of the Alamanni, refers to a *pactum vicissitudinis reddendae*. They were bound to render mutual aid. Can we discover any cause for these approximations, these centripetal movements? Agriculture, in all probability, proved an insufficient solution of the population question, especially if in settled conditions the numbers increased more rapidly. It became necessary therefore for a people to enlarge the area of its habitation by reclaiming the surrounding forestland. You must picture Germany as consisting of small territories each of which was surrounded by a dense impenetrable ring of primeval forest. They were thus divided from and protected against each other by the forest-hedge which formed their hunting-grounds. In the middle of the territory were the separate agricultural allotments of the freemen, all round this was the common pasture land, and beyond this again was the ring of forest. Now what naturally happened as the population increased? More land was required for the separate allotments, and it became necessary to encroach upon the pasture land. But the pasture could not be curtailed with an increasing population, and so it became necessary to encroach upon the forest. The result was that the dense rings of forest, which isolated each state from its neighbours more effectually than the sea severs islands, were reduced to narrow limits with the expansion of the population, and the states were brought into a close proximity which facilitated and promoted political unions, whether intimate or loose. This process of grouping was perhaps favourable to the institution of royalty.

POLITICAL INSTITUTIONS OF THE GERMANS

It will not be amiss to say a few words here, at the very outset, about the political institutions of the Germans – words which apply not merely to the times of Tacitus and of Caesar, with which we are not now directly concerned, but also to the whole time of the migrations which form the subject of the next few lectures. I will not go into any details or discuss vexed questions, but merely emphasise what seems to be the chief feature. I would say in the first place that the whole period of German history before the migrations and during the migrations may be called, from the political point of view, the period of popular freedom. As soon as the German people have formed permanent states in the dismembered Roman Empire a new period of political development begins, a monarchical period. Now I daresay you may be inclined to make an objection to this statement. You may say that in early times (*e.g.* in the time of Tacitus) some of the German states were ruled by kings; there were kingdoms as well as republics; and during the actual period of the migrations nearly every people had a king. This is quite true, and the point on which I wish to insist is that it does not affect my proposition. A German state might have a king or it might not, but in either case it was virtually a democracy. All German states, so far as we know, had to all intents and purposes the same constitution; the political distinction between republic and monarchy has no application to them. Some of them had kings; any of them might at any moment elect a king; but the presence or absence of a king might almost be described as a matter of convenience; it had no decisive constitutional importance. In every German state, whether there was a king or not, the assembly of the freemen was sovran; and that is the main thing to remember. The king not only had no power to legislate or take any political decision without the consent of the assembly, but he had no power to hinder or check what seemed good to the assembly. He was the great executive officer of the state and had the right of summoning the host whenever the assembly had decided on war; also the right of summoning extraordinary meetings of the assembly. But the people who had no king required an executive officer of this kind likewise. Well, they had an officer who was called the graf. The graf had functions and duties corresponding to those of the king. The true distinction then between the German states is not 'republican' and 'monarchical' states, but states with a graf and states with a king. Was the distinction then merely one of name? No, there was one real and important difference. The graf was elected by the assembly, and the assembly might elect anyone they liked. The king was likewise elected by the assembly, but in his case their choice was limited to a particular family, a royal family. In other words, the kingship was hereditary, and the grafship was not. But this hereditary character of the kingship was of a limited kind. When a king died, the office did not devolve on any particular kinsman of his; the sovran people might elect any member of the family they chose; they might refuse to elect a successor at all. There was no fixed successor; the eldest son, *e.g.* , had no greater claim than anyone else. The existence of these kingly families such as the Amals among the East Goths, the Balthas among the West Goths, the Mervings among the Salian Franks, is for us an ultimate fact, behind which with our present knowledge we can hardly penetrate. It is like the existence of the German nobility, the origin of which we have not material to explain. We only know that the kingly family was supposed to be the most ancient of all the families of the folk, and that it traced its origin to a god. And families possessing this right seem to have existed among all the German folks, among those who had no kings as well as among those who had. So that if any kingless folk suddenly resolved that it would be expedient to have a king, they had a family designate within which their choice would fall. It is highly important to realise this absolute nature of the theoretical principle of the ancient German states – namely, the sovranty of the folk, a vital principle which has undergone many modifications, passed through transient eclipses, but has never been extinguished in Europe. But I must go on to point out that, though the king had no independent power, the kingship had importance by virtue of the fact that it *might* become a real power. It was a germ out of which a true royal power might spring – and did spring. The fact that he belonged to a chosen family of high prestige would naturally secure that more special consideration and honour would be shown to the king than to a graf; and a strong man might be able to exercise enormous influence in the assembly by perfectly constitutional means. This was no infringement of freedom, but it might lead ultimately to infringement of freedom.

Now it may be that the growth of these centripetal tendencies, the process of group formation, of which I have spoken, was favourable to the institution of royalty. In the time of Tacitus, states, such as the Saxon, which had a king were exceptional. The motives of this general change of feeling in favour of kingship were no doubt various, and perhaps we cannot determine them with any certainty; but I may point out one consideration. If several states formed a political union and required a head for their common actions, *e.g.* for a war, a king may have seemed the easiest solution. They may have found it easier to agree on giving precedence to the royal family of a particular state than to join together to elect a president. I may observe that within these federal unions each *civitas* had often its own king; this was the case with the Alamanni, and partly with the Franks.

EARLY GOTHIC MIGRATIONS

The events of the fifth century were decisive for the future of Europe. The general result of these events was the occupation of the western half of the Roman Empire, from Britain to North Africa, by German peoples. Now the Germans who effected this occupation were not, with one or two exceptions, the Germans who had been known to Rome in the days of Caesar and Tacitus. They were not West Germans. They were East Germans. The principal of the East German peoples were the Goths, the Vandals, the Gepids, the Burgundians, and the Lombards. There were also the Rugians, the Heruls, the Bastarnae, the Sciri. Most of these peoples believed that they had reached the coast of East Germany from Scandinavia, and this tradition is confirmed by the evidence of names. The best students of German antiquity identify the name of the Goths with that of the Scandinavian Gauts. The Rugians who settled in Pomerania are explained by Rogaland in Norway. The Swedish Bornholm is supposed to be Burgundarholm, the holm of the Burgundians. Of these East German peoples, most were moving slowly through Europe in a generally southward direction, to the Black Sea and the Danube, in the third and fourth centuries. These East German barbarians were still in the stage in which steady habits of work seem repulsive and dishonourable. They thought that laziness consisted not in shirking honest labour but, to quote words of Tacitus, in "acquiring by the sweat of your brow that which might be procured by the shedding of blood". Though the process is not revealed in our historical records, it seems very probable that the defensive wars in which the Emperor Marcus Aurelius, in the third quarter of the second century, was engaged against the Germans north of the Danube frontier – that these wars were occasioned by the pressure of East Germans beyond the Elbe driven by the needs of a growing population to encroach upon their neighbours.

The earliest great recorded migration of an East German people was that of the Goths, about the end of the second century. They moved from their homes on the lower Vistula to the shores of the Black Sea, where we find them in A.D. 214 in the reign of Caracalla.

Before this migration the Goths had formed one people, consisting, like all German peoples, of a number of separate units or *gaus* . I do not think there can be much doubt that it was after their settlement there that they broke up into two great divisions, the Ostrogoths and the Visigoths, and that the motive of the division was geographical. It is easy to imagine how this could have happened, as there can be little doubt that they did not migrate all at once but rather in successive bands. The earlier comers, we might suppose, settled nearer the Danubian lands, in the neighbourhood of the Dniester, and they, in consequence of years of separation, felt themselves in a certain measure distinct when the later comers arrived; and the result was the formation of two groups, distinguished as East and West.

After the whole Gothic nation had been reunited on the shores of the Euxine, the ancient Greek cities of Olbia and Tyras seem to have soon fallen into their hands. We may infer this from the fact that the coinage of those cities comes to an end in the reign of Alexander Severus, who died in A.D. 235. Soon afterwards the Gothic attacks upon the Roman Empire began.

Lecture 2:
The Roman Empire and the Germans

THE GOTHIC ATTACK IN THE THIRD CENTURY A.D. – THE VISIGOTHIC OCCUPATION OF DACIA – OSTROGOTHIC AND VISIGOTHIC SETTLEMENTS – NEW ORGANISATION OF THE EMPIRE

THE GOTHIC ATTACK IN THE THIRD CENTURY A.D.

The recorded attacks of the Goths on the Roman Empire began about A.D. 247. The success of these attacks was due to (1) the internal weakness of the Empire at the time; for it had suffered from a succession of incompetent rulers since the death of Septimius Severus in A.D. 211, and (2) the simultaneous rise of the new Persian Empire, which had given it a very formidable enemy in the east. The Goths now inflicted upon Rome the most grievous and shameful blow that had been struck by northern barbarians since the reign of Augustus when Arminius annihilated the legions of Varus in the forest of Teutoburg. They drew the army of the Emperor Decius into a swamp near the mouths of the Danube, destroyed the army, and slew the Emperor, A.D. 251. Soon afterwards they took to the sea, and sailing forth from the ports of south Russia they became the terror of the cities of the Black Sea, the Marmora, and the Aegean. These ravages did not cease till they attempted a great joint invasion by sea and land, which was decisively repelled by the Emperor Claudius I. (A.D. 269). A despatch is preserved professing to have been written by the Emperor when the foes had been defeated and routed. It runs thus: "We have destroyed 320,000 Goths, we have sunk 2000 of their ships. The rivers are bridged over with shields; the fields are hidden by their bones; no road is free." But the despatch is a later fabrication. The number of 320,000 is a ludicrous exaggeration, as we shall see afterwards when we come to consider the general question as to the numbers of the German invaders and the size of their armies. The achievement of Claudius – who is generally known, in consequence, as Claudius Gothicus – secured peace from the Goths for a long time in the regions south of the Danube; but it would not have done so if he had not been followed by a series of able rulers.

THE VISIGOTHIC OCCUPATION OF DACIA

But meanwhile the Goths were securing a success of a more abiding and important nature than their sensational victory in which a Roman Emperor had perished. They had in fact begun the actual dismemberment of the Empire by penetrating and ultimately occupying one of its provinces – the province of Dacia, north of the Danube, which had been conquered nearly a hundred and fifty years before by the Emperor Trajan, the country which is called Transilvania or Siebenburgen. It was the last European province to be acquired by Rome; it was the first to fall away. No Roman coins, no Roman inscription of date later than about A.D. 256 have been found in Dacia. The Emperor Aurelian, who succeeded Claudius Gothicus in A.D. 270, withdrew the Roman officials and military garrisons from Dacia, and made the Danube once more the frontier of the Empire. Evidently the Goths had been gradually and steadily encroaching on Roman territory for fifteen or twenty years, and Aurelian simply decided to abandon a province which was already virtually lost. No doubt there was a considerable exodus of the provincials when the imperial government withdrew its protection; but we have no trustworthy evidence as to what exactly happened. It is an obscure question, and one on which a great deal of ink has been wasted; for it has been the subject of heated discussions in modern times between the Roumanians and Hungarians. As you know, the Roumanians speak a romance, that is, a Latin language, and they claim to be descendants of the Latin-speaking inhabitants of Roman Dacia, surviving throughout all the vicissitudes of the Middle Ages, throughout all changes of master, since the time of Aurelian, in Transilvania. The Hungarians have strenuously denied this. Transilvania belonged to Hungary up to the recent war, the results of which enabled it to fulfil its aspiration of shaking off the Hungarian yoke and of being united in the free kingdom of Roumania to its eastern neighbours who speak the same language. The view of the Hungarians was that all the romance-speaking peoples north of the Danube were later immigrants from the lands south of the Danube – the Balkan peninsula – who moved northward as late as the twelfth and thirteenth centuries. I can only just call your attention to the existence of this burning question. To discuss it usefully or even intelligibly would take us away to the history of the Danubian lands in the twelfth century. The main thing to point out now is that the Roman period of the history of Dacia or Transilvania comes to an end about A.D. 270 (having lasted for 150 years) and that the Gothic period begins.

Incursions of the Goths continued during the following sixty years. After the Emperor Constantine the Great became sole Emperor in A.D. 324, he gave his attention to the danger, and endeavoured to secure the lower Danube frontier by fortified camps and castles. He built a wall in the north-east corner of Thrace across the region which is now known as the Dobrudzha – a region which in modern times has been disputed between Roumania and Bulgaria. Towards the end of his reign Constantine concluded a forced treaty with the Visigoths. They became *federates* of the Empire; that is, they undertook to protect the frontier and to supply a certain contingent of soldiers to the imperial army in case of wars. In return for this they received yearly subsidies which, theoretically a supply of corn, was actually paid in money, and was technically called *annonae foederaticae* (federal corn supplies). Federal relations of this kind are a standing feature of the whole period during which the German people were encroaching upon the provinces of the Empire from the fourth to the sixth century. They were nearly all *federates* of the Empire, for a longer or shorter time, before they were independent masters of the lands which they had seized. Through this treaty Dacia, occupied by the Visigoths, became nominally a dependency of the Empire, and Constantine might boast that he had in a sense recovered Dacia. The peace lasted for a generation, and during this time the Visigoths, unable to press from the southward or westward, took to more settled habits and began to learn the arts of agriculture.

OSTROGOTHIC AND VISIGOTHIC SETTLEMENTS

The territory of the Goths as a whole, including Visigoths and Ostrogoths, now, towards the middle of the fourth century, extended from the river Theiss or somewhere near it on the west to the river Dnieper on the east. The Visigoths held Dacia, and also parts of what are now Moldavia and Walachia; the Ostrogoths lived in the steppes beyond the Dniester, but we do not know the exact line of division between the two branches of the Gothic race.

These two peoples remained independent of each other. Our sources give us abundant proof that throughout the period up to the end of the fourth century the Visigoths had no king; their constitution was republican. The *gaus* acted in common, and some of the *gau* chiefs had a predominant influence in guiding the council of the nation and were recognised as natural leaders in the case of war; but we must not be misled by the occasional use of the term *rex* , instead of the more usual and proper *judex* , in Roman writers, into supposing that there was a king. Prominent leaders like Athanaric and Fritigern meet us, but they are only *judices* , *gau* chiefs; they are not kings.

On the other hand, royalty was adopted or maintained by the Ostrogoths. We meet an Ostrogothic king before the end of the third century, and in the fourth there arose the prominent figure of Hermanric, of whom more will have to be said presently.

After this peace in the reign of Constantine there is a pause for a generation in the hostilities between the Empire and the East Germans. For about fifty years the Germanic wars of Rome are almost wholly with the West Germans – the Franks and the Alamanni – who give a great deal of trouble on the Rhine frontier. The really grave dangers for Rome in the east will begin in A.D. 378; after which the Emperors will begin to realise how formidable the German peril is.

NEW ORGANISATION OF THE EMPIRE

At this point it will be convenient for us to examine the strength of the Empire itself and compare it with the strength of the Germans. We are greatly handicapped in attempting to form an idea of the actual state of things by not having any accurate statistics of population, and the inferences which we may draw from the very few trustworthy figures we have must be taken with a great deal of reserve.

The first thing to grasp is that in the third century the Empire was declining. This was due not only to external troubles, such as wars with the new Persian Empire which had arisen in the east, but much more to internal dissensions and disruptions, civil wars and contests for the imperial throne. The central government had become weak and almost bankrupt; the various parts of the Roman world were showing tendencies to fall asunder and to set up rulers of their own. One of the most significant symptoms of decay was the depreciation of the coinage.

This state of things was ended by two great Emperors, viz. Aurelian, who obtained the supreme power in 270, and Diocletian, who ascended the throne fifteen years later (285) and reigned for twenty years till 305. In the generation – thirty-five years – which elapsed between the accession of Aurelian, who rescued the Empire at the brink of an abyss, and the end of Diocletian's reign, the administration, the army, and the finances were reorganised. After Diocletian's abdication of power in 305, there were twenty years of trouble – struggles for power among his successors, at the end of which (324) one of the most notable figures in the history of the world, Constantine the Great, emerged victorious. The work of these sovrans completely renovated the Empire; and up to the end of the fourth century it enjoyed a series of able and hard-working rulers who preserved its frontiers virtually intact. There is a striking historical fact which illustrates how the Empire recovered. It relates to the reform of the currency. A new gold standard was introduced by Constantine. You know that we coin 45 sovereigns out of a pound weight of gold. Constantine coined 72 gold pieces to the pound weight. This gold piece was called an aureus or a solidus; and thus in point of value the solidus corresponds to 12s. 6d. Now this standard gold coin, the solidus, was issued from his time up to the eleventh century, by the imperial mints, without any depreciation.

In the third and fourth centuries the Roman Empire extended from the Tyne to the Euphrates. It included all of the lands now known as England and Wales, France, Spain, Italy and Switzerland, Austria and Hungary, the Balkan peninsula, Asia Minor and Syria, and the whole coast lands of North Africa from Egypt to Morocco.

The history of the third century, as already remarked, showed the natural tendency of the parts of this huge heterogeneous empire to fall asunder. The principal line of division was a language line – a line passing through the Balkan peninsula – to the west of which line Latin was spoken generally, and to the east, Greek. Thus the Empire fell naturally into two great sections – a western or Latin section and an eastern or Greek section. This, of course, does not mean that other languages were not spoken too. Coptic was spoken in Egypt, Aramaic in Syria, Celtic tongues in Britain and parts of Gaul, and so on: it means that in the eastern section Greek was the prevailing tongue and the general language of intercourse, and in the western, Latin. The Emperor Diocletian was convinced that the Empire was too huge to be centralised under one sole ruler, and so he made a scheme to place it under two coequal emperors, one ruling the western section, and the other the eastern; each of them to be assisted by a subordinate, or lieutenant, who had not the full imperial title of Augustus, but only the lower title of Caesar. I need not enter upon the details of the scheme, which was highly artificial and remarkably unsuccessful; for it was abandoned by Constantine. But it involved a new imperial centre of government in the east, as well as at Rome; and this led to the great and decisive act of Constantine in establishing a second Rome at Constantinople, A.D. 330.

This division of the Empire into two parts, one mainly Latin, the other mainly Greek, lasted for 150 years; it was for the greater part of that time ruled by two emperors, occasionally it was under one. But throughout all this period there were the two seats of government, one at the old Rome on the Tiber, the other at the new Rome on the Bosphorus; and the two governments, their systems, their organisations, their officials were exactly the same; one was virtually the replica of the other. That was a very remarkable, indeed a unique, experiment in government; an empire ruled not from one centre, but from two foci, through two parallel organisations. The two parts are often loosely spoken of as if they were two distinct Empires – the eastern and the western. That is a mistake against which we must be on our guard. The unity of the two parts was always most carefully maintained. The Roman Empire was always considered one and indivisible. It never entered anyone's head to think of two. The unity was maintained and expressed in various ways, particularly in legislation. When a law was passed at Constantinople, it was issued not merely in the name of the emperor who was ruling there but in the joint names of him and the emperor ruling in the west; and conversely. The old practice of appointing two consuls at the beginning of every year was preserved, and one of them was nominated at Rome and the other at Constantinople.

The renovated Empire received a new organisation, the result of reforms partly due to Diocletian and partly to Constantine. The general result was that for the purposes of civil administration the whole Empire fell into four great sections, two in the west and two in the east, known as prefectures, because each section was governed by a great minister entitled a praetorian prefect, who was responsible solely to the Emperor. The two western prefectures were the Gauls and Italy, but each of these included many lands which we do not now associate with those names. The *Prefecture of the Gauls* included, as well as Gaul, Britain and Spain and the north-west corner of Africa – Morocco. The *Prefecture of Italy* included, as well as Italy, Switzerland and the provinces between the Alps and the Danube, and also the coast lands of North Africa. The two eastern prefectures were the *Prefecture of Illyricum* , which covered the Balkan peninsula, with the exception of Thrace, and was the smallest of the four; and the *Prefecture of the Orient* , which comprised Thrace and Egypt, and all the Asiatic territory that belonged to the Empire.

Each of these prefectures was divided into large districts called dioceses, each of the size of a fair-sized modern state. Thus in the prefecture of the Gauls there were four dioceses: Britain, two dioceses in Gaul, and Spain. And each diocese was under a vicar, who was subject to the praetorian prefect. And in each diocese there were a number of provinces, each under a provincial governor. Thus the whole system of civil government was, roughly speaking, a hierarchy, like a ladder, with the Emperor at the top, the provincial governor at the foot, and the praetorian prefects and the vicars as the intermediate steps – roughly speaking, for there were a number of exceptions and complications which we need not trouble about. For our present purpose what I have said is enough respecting the civil organisation, and its general hierarchial character. Only observe that there are two such systems, two of these hierarchies, one centring at Rome, the other at Constantinople, like two clocks similarly constructed but functioning independently. And it is important to remember that neither of these great civil administrations had any military functions. The separation of civil and military authority was one of the capital features which differentiated the new monarchy of the fourth and following centuries from the earlier empire of Augustus.

It is the military organisation of the Empire which it is of great importance for us to understand, in trying to follow the struggle between the Empire and its German invaders. The principal feature in which the military establishment of the fourth and fifth centuries differed from that of the early Empire was the existence of a mobile army. While all the frontiers were defended by troops permanently stationed in the frontier provinces, distinguished as *limitanei* , there was also a field army which the Emperor could move to any part of his dominion which happened to be threatened whenever war broke out; and these troops, which accompanied the Emperor in his movements and so formed an imperial retinue, or comitatus, were distinguished as *comitatenses* . Thus the military forces consisted of two main classes, the *comitatenses* , who were the most important when there was serious warfare, and the *limitanei* .

A second outstanding feature in the military organisation of the later Empire is the smaller size of the legionary unit. The strength of the old Roman legion, as it had hitherto been, was about 6000 men; and it was associated with a number of cohorts of infantry and squadrons of cavalry, all under the command of the legatus or commander of the legion, so that the legatus had about 10,000 men under him. All this is changed. The old legion of 6000 is broken up into detachments of 1000; new legions that are formed are only 1000 strong; the cohorts and the cavalry squadrons are under separate commanders.

Most important is the separation of the cavalry from the infantry, and its conversion into an independent arm instead of a subordinate one. All these armies were under the supreme command of Masters of Soldiers, *Magistri Militum* . It is usual to translate this term literally; they correspond in rank to what we call Field-Marshals, but they had definite commands, and here the systems in the west and in the east developed rather differently. As this office will constantly be mentioned in these lectures it is necessary to explain briefly its position both in the east and in the west – as it was just before the end of the fourth century.

In the east there were five Masters of Soldiers. Two of these resided at Constantinople and commanded the troops of the field armies stationed in the immediate neighbourhood of the capital. They were distinguished as *Magistri in praesenti* , *i.e.* in immediate attendance on the Emperor. The other three were stationed in the large districts of the east; Thrace, and Illyricum respectively, and commanded the troops stationed in them.

In the *west* it was different. Here we do not find five co-ordinate commanders, but two, *magistri militum in praesenti* , whose headquarters were in Italy; one was commander of the infantry, *magister peditum* , the other of the cavalry, *magister equitum* . But though nominally co-ordinate, the first, the Master of Foot, was much the more important. He had supreme authority not only over the mobile infantry of the west, but also over the commanders of the *limitanei* . Towards the end of the fourth century he acquired superior authority over his colleague the Master of Horse, and thus supreme command of all the military forces of the west, and received the title *magister utriusque militiae* , Master of Both Services. *i.e.* both infantry and cavalry.

This difference in organisation had grave political results. In the west the concentration of military power in the hands of one man made the Master of Both Services the most important and influential minister, the man who really directed the policy of the state, and from the close of the fourth century up to the time when the western half of the Empire had completely passed into the power of the Germans, not only the defence of the Empire but the general management of its affairs was in the hands of a succession of soldiers, Masters of Both Services, who were sometimes a danger to the throne. In the east, on the other hand, there are a few cases, but not many, in which a Master of Soldiers attained to undue power.

Lecture 3:
The Clash of Roman and Barbarian

THE POPULATION OF THE EMPIRE – THE FORCES OF THE EMPIRE AND OF THE BARBARIANS – THE GERMANIC PENETRATION OF THE EMPIRE – HERMANRIC AND WULFILAS – THE ADVENT OF THE HUNS

THE POPULATION OF THE EMPIRE

I explained in the last lecture the general character of the military reforms of Diocletian and Constantine – the most important being the creation of a mobile army. We have now to consider what the strength of the whole military power of the Empire was, both the mobile army and the stationary forces which were arranged along the frontiers and in the most exposed and assailable parts of Roman dominion, and to see how they compared with the forces which were already threatening and were soon to become a very grave danger.

The question of the number of the army leads us to the general question of the population, for which very different figures have been reached. In old days the numbers of the ancient peoples in Greek and Roman times were immensely exaggerated. This was first pointed out in the eighteenth century by David Hume in an epoch-making essay, which showed the impossibility of a great many of the figures given by ancient writers. Gibbon, who fully accepted the conclusions of Hume, made an estimate of the population of the Roman Empire in the first century A.D., and concluded that it was about 120 millions. Nobody now would put it quite so high. A modern computation has assigned the figure 54 millions, which is less than half Gibbon's. Now there is reason to believe that between the first century A.D. and the time of Constantine there was an increase of population, because the increase of town life and civilisation in the provinces of Gaul and Spain and the Danubian countries would naturally bring with it an increase in numbers. I am inclined to think that we shall not be extravagantly astray if we say that in Constantine's age the population was somewhere about 70 millions.

Now with this figure – which is a moderate one – you might expect that in wartime an army could be raised numbering many millions. In a modern state, which has conscription, it used to be calculated that if necessary one-tenth of the total population could be sent into the field, *e.g.* in the late war it used to be calculated that Germany – with a population of 65 millions or more – had 6 or 7 millions to draw on for her army in the field. But conditions in modern warfare are entirely different from those in ancient; because so many of the male population, who would otherwise serve in the actual fighting, are required for making munitions, etc. The conditions in ancient warfare were very different. No substantial portion of the able-bodied men of a country was needed for auxiliary services. Therefore a state of which the free population was, say, a million, could put in the field a far larger fraction than nowadays.

It might, therefore, seem surprising at first to find that the total fighting forces of the Roman Empire (with a population of 70 millions – or even if you lower it and take as the very minimum 55 millions) never reached 1 million. To explain this the first thing to observe is that in the old civilised countries round the Mediterranean Sea the population had become quite useless for military service. They were too highly civilised, and not physically fit enough, on the average, to do hand-to-hand fighting with the uncivilised barbarians. Thus, large parts – and the most populous parts – of the Empire are practically withdrawn from our calculation, for they contributed almost nothing in the form of fighting men to the military strength of Home. So far did this go that in the end it may be said that the only provinces in the interior of the Empire which furnished a constant supply of recruits were the highlands of the Balkan peninsula and the mountainous regions of Asia Minor, for instance Isauria. Otherwise, the army was chiefly recruited from frontier provinces, where there was a population with a large barbarian admixture.

In the third century the army was very largely Illyrian. Diocletian and Constantine both belonged to families of the Balkan peninsula which had risen through military service. In old days foreigners used to be excluded from military service; it was confined to Roman citizens. But at the end of the third century this was given up; foreigners from beyond the limits of the Empire were freely admitted as recruits; while at the same time the principle of the universal liability of citizens was abandoned in practice.

When we examine the way in which the armies were recruited we find that there were four classes of recruits, *i.e.* four sources from which they were drawn.

(1) *The sons of soldiers* : military service was hereditary and the son was bound to follow his father's profession.

(2) *Serfs* : it was a state burden on landed proprietors to supply a certain number of recruits from among their serf tenants.

(3) *Barbarian settlers* : some troops were supplied from the communities of foreign barbarians who were settled in some provinces, especially in east Gaul and north Italy.

(4) *Adventurers* : the most important source of supply was the numerous poor adventurers, both native and foreign, who voluntarily offered themselves to the recruiting officers. Of these adventurers the barbarian volunteers were the most useful and efficient. The Germans who came to enlist, attracted by the pay and the prospect of a career, gradually replaced the Illyrians as the predominant element in the army. Under Roman drill and discipline they became excellent soldiers and rose rapidly to officer rank. Very many of the soldiers who held the highest posts in the last part of the fourth century were of German origin. This is an exceedingly important point. There was in fact a process of Germanisation going on during that century, and it constituted a grave danger. Looking back we can see that the Emperors adopted too liberal a policy in allowing Germans to occupy posts of supreme command. This liberality was due to the desirability of attracting the best men to a career in the imperial service; the Emperor Constantine always showed marked favour to Germans, and Julian reproached him for pampering them. German customs (*e.g.* of elevating an emperor on a shield) made way in the army. The general result was that from the end of the first quarter of the fourth century the German star was gradually rising.

THE FORCES OF THE EMPIRE AND OF THE BARBARIANS

I have now explained how it is that the actual population of the Empire has really no relation at all to its powers of resistance and defence against its enemies. Only a few parts of it made any considerable contribution to the military man-power of the state; and the men who could be got from the Balkan peninsula, the highlands of Asia Minor, the borders of Arabia and Africa, or the lowlands of Batavia had to be supplemented by the recruits who came in great numbers from beyond the Rhine and Danube. We may consider now the actual numbers.

The general result of inquiries into the size of the army after its radical reorganisation by Diocletian and Constantine is that its total strength was between 600,000 and 650,000. This includes both the *comitatenses* and the *limitanei* , the mobile army and the stationary forces who garrisoned the exposed provinces. Of this total strength it is estimated that about one-third (more than 200,000) were in the mobile army and the rest in the garrisons. When you consider the large frontiers which had to be defended, the line of the Rhine, the line of the Danube, as well as the north frontier of Britain in the west, the long frontiers of Africa in the south, the Euphrates, and the Syrian desert in the east, the numbers seem very small. Relatively to the lengths of the frontiers the greater proportion of troops was demanded for the defence of the eastern frontier; for there the enemy was a mighty, well-organised state – the Persian Empire. On the western and northern frontiers the danger came from a number of independent barbarian peoples, who occasionally acted together, but were, even so, far outmatched by the Roman legions in discipline and drill. It has been commonly supposed, however, that this inferiority was more than balanced by their multitude, at least in the case of the East Germans, whose armies have been generally imagined to consist of hundreds of thousands. This idea is fundamentally erroneous, and it is one of the most important points to be quite clear about in studying the barbarian invasions. The enormous figures for the German armies given by many of the chroniclers of the time are absolutely untrustworthy: not only are they on *a priori* grounds impossible, but they are inconsistent among themselves and inconsistent with the statements of those who were most likely to know. When we compare together the figures which we have good reason to consider trustworthy we reach the conclusion that the total number of one of the larger East German nations varied from 80,000 to perhaps 120,000, while that of the smaller peoples varied from 25,000 to 50,000. Now from these totals, which included women and children, the Germans could put a much larger fraction in the field than a civilised state. The military age began somewhat earlier and lasted much longer. A German host could number a quarter or a fifth of the population. And so we find that an army of one of the big East German peoples like the Visigoths, or Ostrogoths, or Vandals, would be as a rule about 20,000 or 25,000, or at most 30,000. And so in most of the battles between imperial troops and East Germans from the fourth to the sixth century we find that the opposing numbers were about 20,000 or so on either side. These facts put a different complexion on the whole history of the German invasions and conquests, and show that the problem of the military defence was not at all in itself hopeless or even superlatively difficult, and that if other elements had not entered in there was no reason why the Empire should have been dismembered. The numbers of the Germans did not make it inevitable.

These facts, as to the comparative size of the Roman armies and the German hosts which were opposed to them, are extremely important to grasp in following the course of the East German invasions, and in most histories they have been either passed over or misrepresented. The second important fact which should be emphasised is the gradually increasing power of the army and the consequent growth of German influence, which at first the Emperors did not realise as a danger. It was, in fact, a sort of peaceful penetration.

I may add that a Germanic element had been filtering into the population of the Empire, in certain districts, in other ways. In the first place, we must remember that the western fringe of Germany had been incorporated with the Empire, in the two Germanic provinces of Gaul. The imperial towns of Cologne, Treves, Mayence, were German. In the second place, many Germans had been induced to settle within the Empire as farmers in desolated tracts of country, after the wars of Marcus Aurelius in the second century. And there were settlements in the Belgic provinces of Germans who had come from beyond the Rhine and received lands in return for which they performed military service, and were organised in communities, and were technically called *laeti*. In many frontier districts there was a considerable German population; because lands were assigned to the soldiers who protected the frontiers (the *limitanei*), and as the army became more and more recruited from Germans, the population of a district on a military frontier might become largely German.

HERMANRIC AND WULFILAS

We may now return to the Goths, and first of all the Ostrogoths. Towards the middle of the fourth century a great warrior king arose among them, by name Hermanric, who seems to have created a Gothic empire which lasted for a few years and secured him a place in Teutonic legend. He is said to have extended his dominion eastward to the Don and also over the Slavonic peoples – Wends and Slovenes – whose habitations stretched from the Upper Vistula to the Dnieper. It is even stated that his power reached to the shores of the Baltic Sea, to the neighbourhood of the old home of the Gothic people. I should not care to guarantee that this empire of Hermanric touched both the Black Sea and the Baltic, stretching from the mouths of the Danube and Dnieper to the mouth of the Vistula. But there is nothing really incredible in the record that he formed one of those transitory barbarian empires of which there have been several other examples in Europe, fabrics which soon and suddenly dissolved because they had no organisation and could not be consolidated, but owed their existence to momentary conditions.

Meanwhile among the Visigoths something of much more importance was happening than the erection of a transitory empire. A Goth of greater ecumenical significance than Hermanric was busy at work. The first introduction of Christianity among a German people outside the Roman Empire, and the first translation of the Bible into a German tongue, mark the beginning of a new era in the history of the Germanic world. The man who accomplished these tasks, and thus became a maker of history, was not of pure Gothic descent. He was sprung from a Cappadocian family which had been carried into captivity among the spoil secured in one of the Gothic raids in the time of Decius or Claudius. But he had been brought up as a Goth, speaking the Gothic tongue, bearing the Gothic name of Wulfilas. Born in the second decade of the fourth century, he was sent while a boy as a hostage to Constantinople, where he came under the influence of Arian Christians, was ordained as a lector, and when he was not more than thirty years of age was consecrated bishop by the great Arian leader, Eusebius of Nicomedia, for the purpose of spreading and organising a Christian church in Gothland. He worked in Dacia and made many converts; but the leaders of the Goths were hostile to Christianity, and their persecutions finally drove him to a course which earned for him from the Emperor Constantine the title of a new Moses. He led his band of Gothic converts out of the pagan land, across the Danube, within the borders of the Empire. They were permitted to settle in Moesia, not far from the ancient city of Nicopolis, and not far from the site where afterwards was to arise the Bulgarian city of Trnovo. They were known as the Lesser Goths – *Gothi Minores*. The Arianism of Wulfilas is of great importance, for it determined the form in which the Goths ultimately accepted Christianity, a form which was, we may suspect, simpler for their intelligence than the difficult doctrine of Nicaea. Important as the work of Wulfilas was in actually making converts, it would have been of very much less moment if he had not achieved two great feats as a means for the accomplishment of his mission. One was the creation of a Gothic alphabet; the other was the translation of the Scriptures into Gothic. Of this Gothic Bible we possess some parts; more than half the Gospels, a great part of the Epistles, some small fragments of the Old Testament. By a strange chance the famous ancient manuscript which contains part of the New Testament, the oldest literary monument of the Teuton, is preserved in Sweden – in that island of Scanzia which the Gothic race remembered as its most ancient home.

The alphabet which Wulfilas invented was based on the Greek, but also partly on the runic alphabet; a fact which shows that the runes were in use among the Goths. But we have another highly interesting record of the use of runes by the Goths in their Dacian period. In 1838 a gold ring (now to be seen in the museum at Bucharest) was found at Petrossan in Little Walachia. It bears a runic inscription, of a dedicatory nature: the word *hailag*, 'holy' is clear, but about the other words there is doubt. The inscription has been interpreted variously as 'holy to the temple of the Goths' or 'Scythia is holy to Woden'. It is in any case a memorial of the pagan period of Gothic history, and of the Gothic period of the history of Dacia.

The Goths were brought into serious collision with the Empire during the civil war which followed upon the death of the Emperor Jovian in A.D. 364. They furnished help to Procopius, the unsuccessful candidate for the Empire, and on the defeat of his cause they incurred the vengeance of his rival Valens, who sent an army against them, notwithstanding their wish to pacify him. The war ended in a complete triumph for the Empire and peace with honour; and it looked as if for many a long year the Danube frontier would be secure.

Meanwhile there was trouble among the Visigoths themselves. They were passing through that painful and exciting crisis which occurs when an old religion is striving to maintain itself against a new religion which is gradually spreading. With the exodus of bishop Wulfilas and his company, Christianity had not died out in Gothland, and the pagan chiefs, especially one of the most prominent, named Athanaric, were intent upon killing it. It made them indignant to see men of their folk withholding sacrifices from the national gods, insulting the images, even burning the sacred groves. And so the blood of martyrs flowed in Dacia. A religious test was instituted. On feast days statues were carried round the wooden dwellings in every village, and whosoever refused to worship was burned alive. You may read about this persecution in the Acts of the martyr Saint Sabas, which preserve a general picture of its character. Besides the religious strife, there was also political strife arising from the jealousy which flamed between the powerful Athanaric and another judge named Fritigern, whose name becomes prominent in the seventies of the fourth century.

THE ADVENT OF THE HUNS

Yet it was a moment at which it behoved the Goths to be united – Visigoths to be united with Ostrogoths, and the two peoples among themselves. Hitherto their wars had been chiefly aggressive. Now they were to be put upon their defence; for a new enemy was already on the horizon, an enemy of Teuton and Roman alike. The nomad hordes known to history as the Huns appeared in the reign of the Emperor Valens west of the Caspian Sea, and swept over southern Russia.

The Huns belonged to the Mongolian division of the great group of races which also includes the Turks, the Hungarians, and the Finns. It may be called the Ural-Altaic race group, and is divided into two great sections, the Uralic and the Altaic. The Uralic section falls into three classes: (1) the Finnic, of which the Finns are the best known representative: (2) the Permian (3) the Ugrian, of which the Hungarians are the most important. The Altaic section falls into several classes, of which one is the Turkish and another the Mongolian. This classification is based on a comparison of the language of these peoples.

I.—URALIC

- **(1) Finnic**
  - **Finns**
  - **Mordvins**
- **(2) Permian**
- **(3) Ugrian**
  - **Hungarians : Ostyaks : Voguls**

II.—ALTAIC

- **(1) Turkish**
- **(2) Mongolian**
- **(3) Manchu-Tungusic**

It is probable that for many generations the Huns had established pastures near the Caspian and Aral Lakes. It may be considered almost certain that their westward movement into Europe was occasioned by political events in northern and central Asia which set in motion new movements among the nomad peoples. Now we know of a great political revolution in Asia in the fourth century which is the probable explanation of the movements of the Huns. Our knowledge, such as it is, of the early history of central Asia is derived from the annals of China. From these records we know that in the third and early fourth centuries the dominant people in these regions was the Sien-pi, and that towards the middle of the fourth century their power was overthrown by the Zhu-zhu, who succeeded them to the dominion of Tartar Asia, and finally founded a great empire extending from the coast of the North Pacific, from Corea to the borders of Europe. It may be supposed that it was events connected with the rise to power of the Zhu-zhu that disturbed the Huns and induced them to move westward.

The name Huns, Greek *ounnoi*, is generally supposed to be a corruption of the word *Hiung-nu* – the name, meaning common slaves, that was given by the Chinese to all the nomadic peoples of Asia. It is important to understand what nomad life meant in the proper sense of the word; for the word is often used in a loose and inaccurate way, as if it simply meant wandering or unsettled. Etymologically, of course, nomad means a grazer. In the strict and proper sense nomad peoples are peoples of pastoral habits who have two fixed lands far apart and migrate between them twice a year regularly like migratory birds. In central Asia northern tracts which are green in summer supply no pasturage in winter, while the southern steppes, which in summer are not inhabitable on account of the drought, afford food to the herds in winter. Hence arises the necessity for two homes.

These nomads are not people who roam promiscuously over a continent. They are herdsmen with two fixed habitations, summer and winter pasture lands, between which they might move for ever, provided the climatic conditions did not change and they were allowed to remain undisturbed by their neighbours. Migrations to new homes would as a rule occur only if strange tribes drove them from their pastures. The successive immigrations of nomads into Europe – of the ancient Scythians; of the Huns; and of all those who come after them – were due, as has already been intimated, to the struggle for existence in the Asiatic steppes, and the expulsion of the weakest. As to those who were forced to migrate: "With an energetic Khan at their head, who organised them on military lines, such a horde transformed itself into an incomparable army, compelled by the instinct of self-preservation to hold fast together in the midst of the hostile population which they subjugated; for however superfluous a central government may be in the steppe, it is of vital importance to a conquering nomad horde outside it." These invading hordes were not numerous; they were esteemed by their terrified enemies to be far larger than they actually were. "But what the Altaian armies lacked in numbers was made up for by their skill in surprises, their fury, their cunning, mobility and elusiveness, and the panic which preceded them, and froze the blood of all peoples. On their marvellously fleet horses they could traverse immense distances, and their scouts provided them with accurate local information as to the remotest lands, and their distances. Add to this the enormous advantage that among them even the most insignificant news spread like wildfire from *aul* to *aul* by means of voluntary couriers surpassing any intelligence department, however well organised." The fate of the conquered populations was to be partly exterminated, partly enslaved, and sometimes transplanted from one territory to another, while the women became a prey to the lusts of the conquerors. The peasants were so systematically plundered that they were often forced to abandon the rearing of cattle and reduced to vegetarianism. This seems to have been the case with the Slavs.

Such was the horde which swept into Europe in the fourth century, encamped in Dacia and in the land between the Theiss and Danube, and held sway over the peoples in the south Russian steppes, the Ostrogoths, Heruls, and Alans. For fifty years after their establishment north of the Danube we hear little of the Huns. They made a few raids into the Roman provinces, and they were ready to furnish auxiliaries from time to time to the Empire. At the time of the death of Theodosius they were probably regarded as one more barbarian enemy, neither more nor less formidable than the Germans who threatened the Danubian barrier. We may conjecture that the organisation of the horde had fallen to pieces soon after their settlement in Europe. No one could foresee that after a generation had passed Rome would be confronted by a large and aggressive Hunnic Empire.

Lecture 4:
The Visigothic Entry into the Empire

THE HUNNIC ATTACK ON THE GOTHS AND ITS SEQUEL – THE BATTLE OF HADRIANOPLE – THE VISIGOTHIC SETTLEMENT – THEODOSIUS AND ALARIC – STILICHO AND THE DIVIDED EMPIRE – ALARIC AT LARGE IN ILLYRICUM

THE HUNNIC ATTACK ON THE GOTHS AND ITS SEQUEL

The first apprisal that the peoples of Europe had of the danger which menaced them through the advance of a new and formidable enemy from Asia was the news of a victory which the Huns had gained over the Alans, a people who lived north of the Caucasus and south of the river Don. This was in the year A.D. 372. The Alans were terror-stricken by the appalling nomads, and a larger portion of the nation fled westward, to be ultimately absorbed in the Germanic world, where we shall meet them again in the story of the migrations. The Huns then continued a westward course across the steppes of south Russia, initiating by their impact a movement the great historical significance of which is that it shuffled and displaced the whole East-Germanic world.

First of all the Ostrogoths were subdued. The empire of Hermanric collapsed before the onrush of the Asiatic shepherds who were to form a greater empire than his: the old king is said to have slain himself in despair. The danger was now at the gates of the Visigoths. The Visigoths, under the leadership of Athanaric, advanced to the Dniester and made a stand, but were utterly defeated. The nation as a whole were seized by panic and firmly believed that there was no safety for them north of the Danube. They determined to withdraw southward beyond that river and seek the shelter of the Roman Empire.

This was a very critical decision: it led to events which determined the course of the history of the Roman Empire. Accordingly they sent an ambassador to the Emperor Valens, who was then staying at Antioch, beseeching him to allow the nation to cross the river and grant them lands in the provinces of the Balkan peninsula. It was the year 376. In the meantime their families abandoned their homes and encamped along the shores of the lower Danube, ready to cross the moment the Romans permitted them. The situation was highly embarrassing for the Emperor and his government. It was unique: they had no experience to guide them in dealing with it. It was pressing; some decision must be come to immediately; there was no time for ripe deliberation. The opinion of ministers and councillors was naturally divided, but it was finally decided to accede to the request of the Goths and to receive them as new subjects on Roman soil. The decision was reached with much hesitation and only after many searchings of heart; but we may be certain that the Emperor and his advisers did not in the least realise or imagine the difficulties of the task to which their consent committed them. To settle peacefully within their borders a nation of perhaps 80,000 or more barbarians was a problem which could be solved only by most careful organisation requiring long preparation. In recent times Europe has had some experience of the enormous difficulties of dealing with crowds of refugees, and of the elaborate organisation which is necessary. Take, for instance, the case of the thousands of Asiatic Greeks who fled from the Turks and sought refuge in European Greece. Here it was simply a case of affording food and shelter to people of the same race, but it taxed the whole resources of the Greek Government to solve it. The problem that met Valens was vastly different and more difficult. Quite suddenly, without any time for thinking out the problem or for any preparation, he was called on to admit into his dominions a foreign nation, of barbarous habits, armed and warlike, conscious of their national unity: to provide them with food, and to find them habitations. The Roman state was highly organised, but naturally there was no organisation to deal with an abnormal demand of this kind, which could not have been anticipated. As might have been expected, when the barbarians crossed the river and encamped in Lower Moesia (Bulgaria) all kinds of difficulties and deplorable incidents occurred. The military and civil officials were quite unequal to coping with the situation, and no wonder. War was the result, a war lasting nearly two years and culminating in A.D. 378 in the great battle of Hadrianople, which is one of the landmarks of history – one of the three most famous disasters that befell Rome in her conflicts with the Germans, the first being the battle of Teutoburg in A.D. 9, when the legions of Varus, the general of Augustus, were annihilated, the second the defeat and death of the Emperor Decius by the Goths in 251. The last Roman historian, Ammianus Marcellinus, ends his work with this battle, and after this year we have to depend – so far as Latin literature is concerned – for the record of the history of the Empire and its German invaders on meagre chronicles, rhetorical verse writers, and incidental notices in ecclesiastical annalists.

THE BATTLE OF HADRIANOPLE

The battle of Hadrianople was fought on August 9; the leader of the Goths was Fritigern; the Romans were commanded by the Emperor Valens himself. Valens made the great error of under-estimating the enemy. He was jealous of the military reputation of his nephew and colleague Gratian, a young man who had succeeded his father Valentinian I. as ruler in the west, and had just gained a signal victory in a war against the Alamanni. Gratian was at this moment marching to help his uncle to crush the Goths, and implored him to take no risks till he arrived and they could meet the enemy with combined forces that would ensure victory. Valens decided not to wait but to win all the glory for himself. The battle resulted in the utter defeat of his legions and his own death. It was a disaster and disgrace that need not have occurred.

It is described at length by Ammianus, but it is curious and very disappointing that, though the historian was a soldier himself, he did not tell his readers definitely the number of the forces on either side. So that we do not know precisely how strong the Goths were, or how strong were the Romans. Gibbon has reproduced the account of Ammianus, and you may conveniently read it in his pages (Chap. XXVI). The point I would emphasise here is the importance of the battle in military history. Hitherto in warfare the Romans had always depended on their infantry. It was their main arm, and in regular battles the cavalry was always considered subsidiary and auxiliary to the legions. Other things being equal, the well-trained legions were almost invincible. In this battle the legions had the novel experience of being ridden down by the heavy cavalry of the German warriors. This was a lesson which showed what cavalry could do; and it had an influence on all subsequent warfare. Between the fourth and the sixth century there was a revolution in the character of the Roman armies and Roman warfare. In the fourth century infantry was the arm on which the Romans still mainly relied, and with which they won their victories in the open field; whereas in the sixth century infantry played a small part in their battles, and victories were won by cavalry. For both these centuries we have detailed descriptions of battles, so that there is no doubt on the question, and these descriptions come from exceptionally good sources, from Ammianus in the fourth and from Procopius in the sixth. Now for the intermediate period, the fifth century, we have not a single good account of any battle written by a contemporary, so that we are not able to trace the change. But it is clear that in the course of that century this change must have come about, to meet the tactics of the East Germans with whom there was constant warfare.

This is a point of considerable interest because until quite late in the Middle Ages, both in west and east, it was cavalry and not infantry with which battles were fought and won. In the fourteenth and fifteenth centuries warfare was again revolutionised by the Swiss pikemen and English archers, who demonstrated that footmen could successfully oppose heavy horse.

THE VISIGOTHIC SETTLEMENT

After their signal triumph in the field the Goths besieged the city of Hadrianople, which they looked forward to capturing easily and plundering. They could not, however, take it; but the open country of the provinces of Thrace was exposed to their depredations for a couple of years. The war was then brought to an end, and there was a general pacification of the Goths. This was achieved through the military activity and the skilful diplomacy of Theodosius the Spaniard, who was coopted Emperor by Gratian at the beginning of A.D. 379 to take the place of the defunct Valens. The chief obstacle to a peaceful arrangement was Fritigern, who stands out in this episode as the moving anti-Roman force. He desired to wrest provinces of the Empire entirely away as his predecessors had wrested Dacia, and to found an entirely independent Gothic state south of the Danube. After his death, however, the Visigoths were induced, through the successes and skilful dealings of Theodosius, to become subjects of the Emperor – not regular provincials and Roman citizens, but allies on a footing of freedom and semi-independence, still remaining a nation but owing definite obligations to the Emperor. Lands in the province of Lower Moesia, the modern Bulgaria, were assigned to them – the same region in which Constantine had settled their Christian fellow-countrymen whom Wulfilas had led out of Dacia. They were to pay no tribute for the land; they were to receive certain pensions from the government; but they were to serve the Empire when needed as federate soldiers under their own chief. The capitulation was concluded in October 382.

In the future shaping of Europe, this series of events had considerable importance: note

(1) The reception of a whole people within the borders of the Empire, as federates, marks a new stage in the process of German encroachment. It strikes what was to be the characteristic note of the dismemberment of the Empire, namely, disintegration from within.

(2) A new destiny is heralded for Dacia and the lands between the Carpathians and the Danube. Dacia had passed from the Dacians to the Romans, from Romans to Teutons; it is now to pass under the rule of the Huns, and the Hun is the forerunner of other non-European conquerors and lords, first the Avars and afterwards the Magyars.

(3) The Gothic people, which had long ago been politically split up into Visigoths and Ostrogoths, becomes now permanently divided. They are parted for ever, each to go its own way; they will never again have to face Rome together. It was much later before the Ostrogoths began to play an important role in history; but they were to some extent mixed up in the troubles of these years. Driven before the Hun, some considerable bands crossed the Danube near its mouth and added to the confusion and disturbances in Thrace. They were defeated by Theodosius, and he, pursuing the same policy as he pursued with the Visigoths, settled them on imperial soil as federates. Not, however, on the frontier, nor in the neighbourhood of the Visigoths, nor even in Europe; he transported them to Phrygia in Asia Minor. They were, however, only a fragment of the nation, of which the greater part seems to have moved westward towards the middle Danube and the frontiers of Pannonia.

THEODOSIUS AND ALARIC

Theodosius fully appreciated the dangers of the Gothic problem, and he pursued unremittingly a policy of conciliation and friendship. He cultivated the friendship of the Gothic chiefs, whom he used constantly to entertain in his palace, and he secured devoted adherents among them, conspicuously Fravitta. There seemed a chance that if this policy were pursued the Goths might gradually become enervated, lose their old restlessness and national pride, and reconcile themselves permanently to the provincial state. But if under the panic inspired by the Hun and the dexterous dealings of Theodosius they seemed to have declined from their old independent spirit, this spirit was far from being yet extinct; and though some of them were fully reconciled to the privileges of belonging to the Empire, there were others who thought otherwise. This division of opinion was openly manifested when a civil war in the Empire seemed imminent in A.D. 392 on the death of Valentinian II. The Gothic chieftains met and held a debate. The question was whether they would fulfil their obligations as federates and serve in the army of Theodosius in the coming war. One party, led by Eriulf, said that they should repudiate their oaths, and that their interests were not the interests of the Empire; the other party which advocated loyalty was led by Fravitta, and the dispute became so hot that in the end Fravitta killed Eriulf. The historical interest of this debate is that it may be considered the prologue to the decisive event which happened a little later, after the death of Theodosius the Great in 395. The Goths had followed Theodosius in his campaign against the usurper Eugenius, but when the great Emperor died, and was succeeded by two very young princes, they reconsidered the position. It proved to be a turning-point in their history. The parliament of the people met and deliberated. Two motives, so we are told, operated. One was dislike and distrust of the new Emperors or rather of their advisers; the other was the apprehension that if they continued as they were they would become enervated and would decline. In any case it was felt that preparation must be made for emergencies; and that the best preparation was unity and a leader. Accordingly the Visigoths chose a king. They had a family marked out to furnish a king whenever a king should be chosen, the Balthas or Bolds, and their choice fell on Alaric the Bold. This chieftain was now about thirty years old. He had been born in Peuce, an island at the mouth of the Danube. He had taken part in the recent civil war, marching with Theodosius as captain of Gothic federate troops, and had returned with high hope of promotion in the Roman army. He aspired, like other German leaders, to the post of a Roman general commanding legions. He built on promises made by Theodosius, but when that Emperor died the promises were not fulfilled, and Alaric was bitterly disappointed. Another course was opened to him when he accepted the kingship of his people in 395: he was to be a foe and not a defender of the Empire; first in the Balkan peninsula and afterwards in Italy.

STILICHO AND THE DIVIDED EMPIRE

Theodosius had left his two sons under the protection of Stilicho, his most trusted general, to whom he had given in marriage his sister Serena, so that Stilicho was the uncle by marriage of the two young Emperors. Their names were Arcadius and Honorius; both of them were weak (but not vicious), and the younger, Honorius, simply feeble-minded. To Arcadius fell the rule of the eastern portion of the Empire; he reigned at Constantinople. To Honorius fell the government of the western portion; Rome was his seat of government, but he generally resided at Milan. The government of the west was entirely in the hands of Stilicho, who was the Master of Both Services, and thus – as I explained before – controlled completely the entire military establishment of that portion of the Empire. For the next thirteen years Stilicho would be the most powerful man in the Roman world.

The power of Stilicho would not turn out to the advantage of the Empire ultimately. He was a German by descent; his ancestors on his father's side were Vandals. He was one of the series of able Germans who in the second half of the fourth century had risen to the highest military commands, conspicuous among whom were Merobaudes, Bauto, and Arbogastes, who was the immediate predecessor of Stilicho as Master of Both Services, and the murderer of Valentinian II. Germans now were coming very close to the throne. Stilicho, as we saw, married the sister of Theodosius, and Bauto was the father of the lady Eudoxia, who became the wife of Arcadius. Thus their son, the Emperor Theodosius II., had German blood in his veins.

The policy of the Emperors of elevating Germans to supreme posts in the army was unfortunate in its consequences. The policy was due to the necessity of making the service attractive to the ablest by the prospect of great power and wealth. But, as it turned out, it was disastrous. Especially was it a singular misfortune that just at the moment when the Empire had to be defended not only against the Germanic peoples who were continually knocking at its gates, but also against Germanic peoples who had already gained admittance, and when there were two incapable sovrans, its defence should have devolved upon a German, attached though that German was both to the Empire and to the reigning family.

The fact that in the critical moment which the Roman state had now reached the two chief actors – the defender as well as the aggressor – Stilicho and Alaric – are both Germans best illustrates one of the many features in the history of the fourth century – a gradual Germanisation within the Empire. Yet formally – and this is important to remember, and equally characteristic of the situation – formally it is not correct to speak at this juncture of an attack upon the Empire on the part of Alaric and the Visigoths. If Alaric had been told that he was attacking the Empire and seeking to destroy it he would have repudiated the suggestion. The existence of the Roman Empire was almost a necessity of thought to Alaric and all his contemporaries. They might ravage the Roman world and try to force the government to do and give what they wanted; but all their ambitions were consistent with its continuance. The Goths aimed at gaining a satisfactory position within its borders; they did not feel like hostile outsiders. The attitude of the Goths, and of the Germans generally, towards the Empire was the direct result of the gradual Germanisation. They did not regard it as a foe to be defeated, but as a great institution in which they had a natural right to have a place, seeing that men of their own race had already a large part in it. Their hostilities, they might have argued, were less like the hostilities of external enemies and rivals, than of disfranchised classes struggling to wrest for themselves a place in the body politic. Alaric did not feel a stranger in a realm in which Germans held the highest posts and might even intermarry with ladies of the imperial house; a realm for which he had himself performed military service.

ALARIC AT LARGE IN ILLYRICUM

After Alaric had been elected king of the Visigoths, he lost no time in striking. He held an assembly, and in it a resolution was taken to march forth and ravage the other provinces of the Illyrian peninsula.

The career of Alaric, which is in some ways one of the strangest episodes in the dismemberment of the Empire, is enveloped in much obscurity. I refer not only to the chronological gaps in the record of what he actually did, but also to his motives and his policy. For fifteen years he was making history, and yet there is almost always room for some uncertainty as to his designs. Now we have a record, which I have mentioned already, that Alaric had aspired to a high command in the Roman army. In other words his original ambition had been to rise to the eminence of power and dignity of a Merobaudes or a Stilicho. The record is so probable that we may readily accept it; and we infer that his acceptance of the kingship of the Visigoths was in some sense a *pis aller* . Remember that the dignity of a German king must have greatly declined in value, in the eyes of the Germans themselves, through long familiarity with the far greater prestige of the Empire. They had become accustomed to see of how little account a *rex* was in the eyes of a praetorian prefect or even of a provincial governor. Starting, then, with the fact that a career in the imperial service had been Alaric's ambition, I think that the clue to his work is that he had claims and ambitions for himself, besides, and distinct from, his claims and designs for his people. For his people the only thing which they desired or claimed was more territory or larger pensions, and if that had been the only object he might probably soon have obtained it. But he had at first another aim for himself personally, and when no place was found for him either in the east or in the west, he could not rest content in the obscure peace of Moesia, but made his power felt as a hostile force in the Empire which had not satisfied his ambitions. That is the way in which I read the beginning of Alaric's career.

The Goths spread desolation in Thrace and Macedonia and advanced close to the walls of Constantinople. The government of Arcadius had no troops sufficient to take the field against them. For the legions of the field army which were usually stationed in the neighbourhood of the capital had accompanied Theodosius to the west when he had marched against the rebel Eugenius, and had not yet returned. Stilicho, however, was already preparing to lead them back in person. He considered that his own presence in the east was necessary; for, besides the need of dealing with the barbarians, there was a political question in which he was deeply interested touching the territorial division of the Empire between its two sovrans. It is not possible to understand the history of the following years without having the importance of this question constantly in mind – it is the question of Illyricum.

The Prefecture of Illyricum had been before the reign of Theodosius the Great subject to the ruler of the west. It included Greece and the central Balkan lands of the Danube. The only part of the peninsula governed from Constantinople was Thrace. But under Theodosius the Great the prefecture was transferred from the west to the east, and the new line of division between the two halves of the Empire was a line running from Belgrade westward along the river Save and then turning southward along the river Drina and reaching the coast of the Adriatic at a point near Scutari. It was assumed at Constantinople that this arrangement would remain in force and that the prefecture would remain under the control of the eastern government. But Stilicho declared that it was the will of Theodosius that his sons should revert to the older arrangement, and that the authority of Honorius should extend to the borders of Thrace, so that only the Prefecture of the East should be left to Arcadius. Whether his assertion was true or not, his policy meant that the western realm, in which he himself was unquestionably supreme, should have a marked predominance over the eastern section of the Empire.

To change the division of Illyricum at the expense of the east was a political aim of which Stilicho never lost sight, and it is the clue to his career after the death of his master. The importance of Illyricum did not lie in its revenues, but in its men. From the third to the sixth century the most useful troops in the imperial army were recruited from the highlands of Illyricum and Thrace. It may well have seemed that a partition assigning the whole of the great recruiting ground to the east was unfair to the west. Events proved that the legions at Stilicho's disposal were quite inadequate to the defence of the west, and therefore it was not unnatural that he should have aimed at bringing the western lands of the Balkan peninsula back under the rule of the western government.

This was a question on which the government of Arcadius was not likely readily to yield, controlled as it was by a powerful and ambitious minister, Rufinus, the Praetorian Prefect of the East. Stilicho took the precaution of bringing with him some western legions of his own, as well as the eastern troops whom he was to restore to Constantinople. In Thessaly he came face to face with Alaric and his Visigoths, who had reached this country in a devastating march from the neighbourhood of Constantinople. He was just preparing to smite the Goths when messengers arrived from Arcadius, commanding him to send the eastern troops on, but himself to return to Italy. Stilicho obeyed the command, and thereby sacrificed Greece. For there is no doubt that he could easily have crushed the Goths and rendered Alaric harmless. But he sent the troops of Arcadius back to Constantinople under a captain named Gaïnas, a Goth. We cannot say whether he came to any understanding with Alaric; but he certainly had an understanding with Gaïnas. When this officer and his army arrived at Constantinople, Arcadius came forth to receive them a few miles from the city, and he was accompanied by his great minister, the Praetorian Prefect Rufinus. The soldiers of Gaïnas assassinated Rufinus, and there is no doubt that Stilicho had plotted this murder with Gaïnas. Indeed Stilicho took no trouble to conceal his complicity in the act. After the fall of Rufinus, a eunuch named Eutropius, who was the Emperor's chamberlain, became the most powerful minister at Constantinople.

This event happened at the end of A.D. 395. Meanwhile Alaric and his host moved southward into Greece. They occupied Piraeus, the port of Athens, but spared Athens itself; they plundered the great temple of Eleusia, and their visit marks the end of the celebration of the Eleusinian mysteries. Then they passed into the Peloponnese, where all the chief towns fell before them. The Peloponnese was in their hands for more than a year, the year 396, and the government of Arcadius made no attempt to dislodge them. Then in the spring of A.D. 397 Stilicho intervened again. He landed in the Peloponnese and confronted Alaric in Elis. There was some fighting, perhaps only make-believe. In any case Stilicho came to some agreement with Alaric and allowed him again to go free as in Thessaly. It seems that the eastern government intervened, and an arrangement was made that Alaric should withdraw to Epirus and should receive the title which he had long coveted, that of Master of Soldiers in Illyricum. Stilicho's expedition was futile. He was obliged to return hastily to Italy on account of the outbreak of a very serious Moorish revolt in Africa. But his presence with an army in the Peloponnese had caused great anger at Constantinople, and the eastern government declared him a public enemy.

Lecture 5:
The Raiding of Italy and Gaul

ALARIC TURNS FROM EAST TO WEST – THE PUZZLE OF STILICHO'S BEHAVIOUR – THE BREAKING OF THE RHINE FRONTIER – DEATH OF STILICHO

ALARIC TURNS FROM EAST TO WEST

We left Alaric in Epirus, in the summer of 397. He had been appointed by the government of Constantinople to the high command of Master of Soldiers in Illyricum, and for the time being his ambitions seem to have been satisfied. During the next four years he remained quiescent, and his presence, so far as our records go, seems hardly to have affected the course of history. We are not even quite sure where his people lived at this time, whether in Epirus or in regions nearer the Danube; possibly they were still mainly in their old homes in Moesia. In any case they did not disturb the Empire before 401. Till this year Alaric's designs apparently did not travel outside the Balkan peninsula, but from this time onward his eyes were turned towards the west.

The causes of this change are not indicated in our authorities, but there is one thing which had probably something to do with it, a thing which is even in itself of very great historical importance. The Gothic soldier Gaïnas, who was responsible for the murder of Rufinus, the praetorian prefect, aspired to being in the east what Stilicho was in the west. He rebelled against the government of Arcadius, forced it to yield to his demands, and for about six months exercised a power that was almost supreme in Constantinople. But there was a very strong and determined anti-German party there, and they gained a decisive victory over Gaïnas and his Gothic troops; and the danger, which at one moment seemed serious, of a Germanisation of the government in the east was averted. Now we may take it that Alaric had found support in the party of Gaïnas, and that the fall of that general in A.D. 400 altered his prospects. At all events, it was in the year 401 that he determined to bring pressure to bear, not upon Constantinople, but on the government in Italy. It is not improbable that he demanded a settlement and lands for his people in some of the northern provinces of the Prefecture of Italy, perhaps in Noricum.

But in threatening the west he did not act alone. He acted simultaneously, though there is no reason to think that he acted in concert, with a somewhat mysterious German named Radagaisus. Radagaisus was probably an Ostrogoth; he may have been one of the Ostrogoths who had been allowed to settle in Pannonia by Gratian; but perhaps he and his followers had taken up their abode just beyond the frontiers, on the other side of the Danube. Towards the end of 401 Radagaisus and a host of barbarians invaded Raetia and at the same time marched to the borders of Italy. It was a critical moment for Stilicho, on whom the defence of Italy devolved. He marched into the Alpine regions of Raetia against Radagaisus, who seems to have moved first, and he was successful in repelling and driving out the invaders. Then he led his troops back south of the Alps to deal with Alaric and the Visigoths, who had already been three months in north Italy, meeting no resistance and causing the utmost consternation among the Italians, who had long been accustomed to regard Italian soil as inaccessible to foreign invasion. The young Emperor Honorius was trembling in Milan, and thought of fleeing to Gaul. Alaric had captured Aquileia and all the towns of Venetia, and was already beginning a siege of Milan, hoping to seize the Emperor's person, when Stilicho arrived just in time to relieve it. Alaric raised the siege and marched westward into Piedmont, followed by Stilicho. Finally he halted at Pollentia on the river Tanarus, and gave battle. This was not the only battle that Alaric fought against the forces of the Empire, but it was far the most famous. It was fought on Easter Day in A.D. 402 and was indecisive, but strategically it was a victory for the imperial army and Stilicho.

Alaric's position became untenable, and he marched into Tuscany. Some members of his family fell into the hands of the Romans. He was glad to make terms with Stilicho. We do not know precisely what the conditions were, but it was certainly arranged that the Visigoths should leave Italy, and there was probably an understanding that they should afterwards assist Stilicho in carrying out the plan on which he was set, of annexing the Prefecture of Illyricum to the Western Empire. Alaric left Italy by the way he had come. But for more than a year he lingered near the borders of the peninsula in Istria and Dalmatia; and then becoming impatient, and perhaps being pressed by want of provisions, he again forced his way into Italy, but was met by Stilicho near Verona and decisively repelled. This was in the autumn of 403. A new agreement was made, and Alaric seems to have withdrawn immediately to his old station in Epirus.

The Italian enterprise of Alaric had been a failure. Whatever he wanted, he had not got it. But though a failure it was an important episode in Alaric's career, and that career occupies an important, even unique, place in the story of the breaking up of the Empire.

THE PUZZLE OF STILICHO'S BEHAVIOUR

Wonder has often been expressed that Stilicho did not follow up the check he inflicted on the Goths at Pollentia with more energy, and that when he defeated them again next year at Verona he again let them go. Why did he not strike harder, why did he leave the enemy free to organise new aggressions and prefer new demands? Stilicho was clearly determined to hold the frontiers of the western provinces against the inroads of the barbarians; he did not spare himself in attempting to perform this duty. How are we to explain his indulgence towards the Visigoths and his leniency, which his Roman contemporaries regarded as culpable?

The formation of barbarian settlements within the Empire had been a recognised principle of policy for two hundred years, and it was difficult for anyone in Stilicho's day to conceive that it would ultimately lead to the disappearance of the imperial authority. Such an idea was equally beyond the visions of Stilicho and of Alaric. We can see plainly that the federate Germans within the Empire were as powerful a force of disruption, and more insidious, than the Germans without the Empire. But for Stilicho there was a gulf fixed between the outside enemies who attacked the frontier and the inside strangers who were linked to the Empire. Against the former he was ready to be ruthless, but the latter were on a different footing; they were part of the system of the Empire, they were to be managed rather than crushed. In the heart of Stilicho this feeling would naturally have been stronger than in a minister of Roman descent; for Stilicho was himself sprung from such federate settlers. But beside this general consideration there can be no doubt that there was a particular motive. It was Stilicho's object to keep Alaric within the precincts of the eastern half of the Empire. He was not ready to admit Gothic settlements within the Prefecture of Italy; but the existence of a strong Gothic power in Illyricum suited his policy, and he foresaw that Alaric might in certain eventualities be a useful ally. I have already touched on the hostility which prevailed between the courts and ministers of the two sons of Theodosius, and pointed out that one of the difficulties and causes of discord was the boundary between the two realms. Stilicho and the western government desired to draw the line of division farther east, and to add to the dominion of Honorius, if not the whole Prefecture of Illyricum, at all events the northern portion of it – corresponding to Serbia and the western part of Bulgaria. When the moment should come for carrying the wish into effect, Alaric's aid might be invaluable. The policy of Stilicho, therefore, was not to crush Alaric, but to keep him quiet, by negotiations and management, in the Illyrian provinces of Arcadius. And for nearly five years after the battle of Verona, 403-408, Alaric and his Goths dwelled under their rooftrees in Epirus, without attempting any new enterprise. In 405 Alaric's former ally Radagaisus descended with a great horde upon Italy; but Alaric took no part in this campaign, and Stilicho's strategy destroyed the barbarians at Fiesole without a battle. Here Stilicho showed that he had no scruples in crushing a German foe.

THE BREAKING OF THE RHINE FRONTIER

The invading of Italy by Alaric and Radagaisus led to some important results. The Emperor Honorius had been very nearly captured at Milan and he decided that it was not a safe place for him to live in. So he withdrew his residence and court to Ravenna on the Adriatic, a place much easier to defend against enemies and in the midst of the marshes, and from which, if the worst came, he could easily escape by sea and find refuge at Constantinople. The change was made soon after the battle of Pollentia in 402, and for five centuries Ravenna was politically the most important place in Italy, next to Rome itself.

That was one consequence of these invasions at the beginning of the fifth century. Another result was that a new disposition of the military forces of the Empire was rendered necessary; and this led inevitably to an event which was fraught with the most far-reaching and fatal consequences to the Empire, an event that occurred in A.D. 406.

Italy was no longer safe, and the troops which should have been holding the Rhine frontier were wanted for the defence of Italy and the imperial capital. In the year 406 the Rhine barrier was practically open, and the opportunity was seized by a vast mixed horde of barbarians who streamed across. This was one of the greatest events in the period of the Germanic wanderings, and it brought a larger and more sudden change in the western province than any other single barbarian movement. It begins a new period in the history of the West German peoples who dwelled along the Rhine. Had it not been for the existence of the Roman power, their natural expansion would have long ago carried them westward to the Atlantic; but they had been curbed by the Roman barrier. Now at length the Roman barrier is giving way, and the West Germans will have a chance of encroaching. The important historical fact that I would emphasise is that this change was not brought about by the West Germans themselves. It was brought about by the East Germans; and brought about through operations not on the Rhine frontier itself, but in another part of Europe. It was the movements of Alaric and his Visigoths, of Radagaisus the Ostrogoth and his mixed hosts, that forced the Roman government to denude the Gallic frontier in order to defend Italy. These were the principal causes and consequences of Alaric's first Italian campaign and the invasions of Radagaisus. The imperial power in Gaul receives a blow from which it will never recover; the influence of Italy upon Gaul is reduced and will continue to diminish.

But not only was it owing to the *East* German movements in another quarter that the Rhine frontier was left inadequately protected, but the first great irruption through the barrier was a movement which was principally *East* German. Of those hordes of barbarians who streamed across the river at the end of 406 the most important were East German peoples. The invaders consisted of *four* peoples, two of which, the most numerous and important, were Vandals. The third were Sueves; and the fourth were of non-Germanic race, the Alans. The Vandals were East Germans. They had come, like the Goths, southward from the Baltic shores.

The name Vandal was applied not to a single people, but to several closely related peoples. The two peoples which concern us were the Asdings and the Silings. The Asdings took the name of Vandals, which was doubtless an older name of their race. The Silings also took the same name, and some time in the third century a considerable number of them, though not the whole people, migrated westward and appeared in the time of the Emperor Probus on the river Main.

The Asding Vandals were then neighbours of the Visigoths of Dacia, and throughout the fourth century there were hostilities between them, which finally resulted in a great defeat of the Vandals. And for a generation we do not hear of them. But about the year 400 their population had increased; their settlements no longer sufficed for their numbers – of this we have explicit evidence. So they determined to migrate, and in 406 took the decisive step at the favourable moment when the Roman troops had been withdrawn from the Rhine. They were joined by a West German people, probably the Quadi, who had belonged to the old Suevic confederacy and took the name of Sueves; also by a non-Germanic people, the Alans, whom we already met driven westward before the Huns. When they approached the Rhine they were further joined by their kinsfolk the Vandal Silings, who, as we saw, had formed a home on the Main. All four peoples poured across the Rhine.

This event was decisive for the future history of western Europe, though the government of Ravenna had little idea what its consequences would be. But Stilicho was at least bound to hasten to the rescue of the Gallic provincials. Instead of doing this, however, he busied himself (A.D. 407) with his designs on Illyricum which the invasion of Radagaisus had compelled him to postpone. The unfriendliness which had long existed between the eastern and western courts had come to a crisis when the ecclesiastics whom Honorius had sent to remonstrate with his brother on the treatment of Chrysostom were flung into prison. It was a sufficient pretext for Stilicho to close the Italian ports to the ships of the subjects of Arcadius and break off all intercourse between the two realms. Alaric was warned to hold Epirus for Honorius; and Jovius was appointed, in anticipation, Praetorian Prefect of Illyricum. Stilicho was at Ravenna, making ready to cross the Hadriatic, when a report reached him that Alaric was dead. It was a false report, but it caused delay; and then came the alarming news that a certain Constantine in Britain had been proclaimed Emperor and had crossed over to Gaul. Once again the design of Stilicho was thwarted. He might look with indifference on the presence of barbarian foes in the provinces beyond the Alps, but he could not neglect the duty of devising measures against a rebel.

DEATH OF STILICHO

Alaric cared not at all for the difficulties of his paymaster, and chafed under the intolerable delay. Early in A.D. 408, threatened perhaps by preparations which the eastern government was making to reassert its authority in Illyricum, he marched northward and followed the high road from Sirmium to Emona. He halted there, and, instead of marching across the Julian Alps to Aquileia and Italy, he turned northward by the road which led across the Loibl Pass to Virunum. Here in the province of Noricum he encamped, and sent an embassy to Rome demanding compensation for all the trouble he had taken in the interest of the government of Honorius. Four thousand pounds of gold (£180,000) was named. The Senate assembled, and Stilicho's influence induced it to agree to the monstrous demand. The money was paid to Alaric, and he was retained in the service against the usurper in Gaul.

But Stilicho's position was not so secure as it seemed. His daughter, the Empress Maria, was dead, but Honorius had been induced to wed her sister Aemilia Materna Thermantia, and Stilicho might think that his influence over the Emperor was impregnable, and might still hope for the union of his son with Placidia. But any popularity he had won by the victory over Gildo, by the expulsion of Alaric from Italy, by the defeat of Radagaisus, was ebbing away. The misfortunes in Gaul, which had been occupied by a tyrant and was being plundered by barbarians, were attributed to his incapacity or treachery, and his ambiguous relations with Alaric had only resulted in a new danger for Italy. It was whispered that his designs on eastern Illyricum only covered the intention of a triple division of the Empire, in which his own son Eucherius should be the third imperial colleague. Both he and his wife Serena were detested by the pagan families of Rome who still possessed predominant influence in the capital. Nor was his popularity with the army unimpaired. While he and Honorius were at Rome in the spring of A.D. 408, a friend warned him that the spirit of the troops stationed at Ticinum was far from friendly to his government.

Honorius was at Bononia (Bologna), on his way back to Ravenna, when the news of the death of his brother Arcadius reached him (May). He entertained the idea of proceeding to Constantinople to protect the interests of his child-nephew, Theodosius; and he summoned Stilicho for consultation. Stilicho dissuaded him from this plan, urging that it would be fatal for the legitimate Emperor to leave Italy while a usurper was in possession of Gaul. He undertook himself to travel to the eastern capital, arguing that during his absence there would be no danger from Alaric, if he were given a commission to march against Constantine. The death of Arcadius had presented to Stilicho too good an opportunity to be lost for prosecuting his design on Illyricum. Honorius agreed, and official letters were drafted, signed, and sent, on the one hand to Alaric instructing him to restore the Emperor's authority in Gaul, and, on the other hand, to Theodosius regarding Stilicho's mission to Constantinople.

But Stilicho's career was at an end. The Emperor proceeded to Ticinum (Pavia), and there a plot was woven for the destruction of the powerful and unsuspecting minister. Olympius, a palace official, who had opportunities of access to Honorius on the journey, let fall calumnious suggestions that Stilicho was planning to do away with Theodosius and place his own son on the eastern throne. At Ticinum he sowed the same suspicions among the troops, who were discontented and mutinous. His efforts brought about a military revolt, in which nearly all the highest officials who were in attendance on the Emperor, including the Praetorian Prefects of Italy and Gaul, were slain (August 13).

The first thought of Stilicho – when the confused story of these alarming occurrences reached him at Bononia, and it was doubtful whether the Emperor himself had not been killed – was to march at the head of the barbarian troops who were with him and punish the mutineers. But when he was reassured that the Emperor was safe, reflexion made him hesitate to use the barbarians against Romans. His German followers, conspicuous among them Sarus the Goth, were eager to act and indignant at the change of his resolve. He went himself to Ravenna, probably to assure himself of the loyalty of the garrison; but Honorius, at the instigation of

Olympius, wrote to the commander instructions to arrest the great Master of Soldiers. Stilicho under cover of night took refuge in a church, but the next day allowed himself to be taken forth and imprisoned on the assurance that the imperial order was not to put him to death, but to detain him under guard. Then a second letter arrived, ordering his execution. The foreign retainers of his household, who had accompanied him to Ravenna, attempted to rescue him, but he peremptorily forbade them to interfere, and was beheaded (August 22, A.D. 408). His executioner, Heraclian, was rewarded by the post of Count of Africa. His son Eucherius was put to death soon afterwards at Rome, and the Emperor hastened to repudiate Thermantia, who was restored a virgin to her mother. The estates of the fallen minister were confiscated as a matter of course. There had been no pretence of a trial, his treason was taken for granted; but after his execution there was an inquisition to discover which of his friends and supporters were implicated in his criminal designs. Nothing was discovered; it was quite clear that if Stilicho meditated treason he had taken no one into his confidence.

The fall of Stilicho caused little regret in Italy. For thirteen and a half years this half-Romanised German had been master of Western Europe, and he had signally failed in the task of defending the inhabitants and the civilisation of the provinces against the greedy barbarians who infested its frontiers. He had succeeded in driving Alaric out of Italy, but he had not prevented him from invading it. He had annihilated the host of Radagaisus, but Radagaisus had first laid northern Italy waste. It was while the helm of state was in his hands that, as we have yet to see, Britain was nearly lost to the Empire, and Gaul devastated far and wide by barbarians who were presently to be lords in Spain and Africa. The difficulties of the situation were indeed enormous; but the minister who deliberately provoked and prosecuted a domestic dispute over the government of eastern Illyricum, and allowed his policy to be influenced by jealousy of Constantinople, when all his energies and vigilance were needed for the defence of the frontiers, cannot be absolved from responsibility for the misfortunes which befell the Roman state in his own lifetime and for the dismemberment of the western realm which soon followed his death. Many evils would have been averted, and particularly the humiliation of Rome, if he had struck Alaric mercilessly – and Alaric deserved no mercy – as he might have done more than once, and as a patriotic Roman general would not have hesitated to do. The Roman provincials might well feel bitter over the acts and policy of this German, whom the unfortunate favour of Theodosius had raised to the supreme command. When an imperial edict designated him as a public brigand who had worked to enrich and to excite the barbarian races, the harsh words probably expressed the public opinion.

The death of the man who had been proclaimed a public enemy at Constantinople altered the relations between the two imperial governments. Concord and friendly co-operation succeeded coldness and hostility. The edict which Stilicho had caused Honorius to issue, excluding eastern traders from western ports, was rescinded. The Empire was again really, as well as nominally, one. The Romans of the west, like the Romans of the east, had shown that they did not wish to be governed by men of German race, and the danger did not occur again for forty years.

Lecture 6:
The Visigoths in Italy and Gaul

THE SACK OF ROME – DEATH OF ALARIC – ATAULF AND GALLA PLACIDIA – WALLIA AND THE SETTLEMENT IN GAUL

THE SACK OF ROME

The fall of Stilicho was the signal for the Roman troops to massacre with brutal perfidy the families of the barbarian auxiliaries who were serving in Italy. The foreign soldiers, 30,000 of them, straightway marched to Noricum, joined the standard of Alaric, and urged him to descend on Italy.

The general conduct of affairs was now in the hands of Olympius, who obtained the post of Master of Offices. He was faced by two problems. What measures were to be taken in regard to Constantine, the tyrant who was reigning in Gaul? And what policy was to be adopted towards Alaric, who, from Noricum, was urgently demanding satisfaction of his claims? The Goth made a definite proposal, which it would have been wise to accept. He promised to withdraw into Pannonia if a sum of money were delivered to him, and hostages interchanged. The Emperor and Olympius declined the proffered terms, but took no measures for defending Italy against the menace of a Gothic invasion.

I will not enter into a detailed narrative of the events of the two following years, 408-410 – the three sieges of Rome by the Goths, the intrigues of the Roman ministers, the elevation and discrownment of Alaric's Emperor Attalus. I will only emphasise the points which bear upon the purpose and policy of Alaric. He still aimed at two things. He wanted a goodly and permanent territory within the diocese of Italy or Illyricum for his people; and he wished for a high military command for himself. But the first of these two aims was now by far the more important. He did not yet think of planting Gothic settlements in the heart of the Italian peninsula, but rather in the northern parts of the Prefecture of Italy; and he hoped to establish a Visigothic kingdom dependent upon the Empire. His purpose in marching through Italy and attacking Rome was to put pressure on the imperial government to give in to his demands.

Alaric acted promptly. In the early autumn of A.D. 408 he crossed the Julian Alps, and entered Italy for the third time. He marched rapidly and unopposed, by Cremona, Bononia, Ariminum, and the Flaminian Way, seldom tarrying to reduce cities; for this time his goal was the capital itself. The story was told that a monk appeared in his tent and warned him to abandon his design. Alaric replied that he was not acting of his own will, but was constrained by some power incessantly urging him to the occupation of Rome. At length he encamped before its walls, and hoped soon to reduce by blockade a city which had made no provision for a siege. His hopes were well founded. The Senate was helpless and stricken with fear. The Visigothic host hindered provisions from coming up the Tiber from Portus, and the Romans were soon pressed by hunger and then by plague. The streets were full of corpses. Help had been expected from Ravenna; but, as none came, the Senate at length decided to negotiate. There was, however, a curious suspicion abroad that the besieging army was not led by Alaric himself, but by a follower of Stilicho who was masquerading as the Gothic king. In order to assure themselves on this point, the Senate chose as one of the envoys John, the chief of the imperial notaries, who was personally acquainted with Alaric. The envoys were instructed to say that the Romans were prepared to make peace, but that they were ready to fight and were not afraid of the issue. Alaric laughed at the attempt to terrify him with the armed populace of Rome, and informed them that he would only desist from the siege on the delivery of all the gold, silver, and movable property in the city, and all the barbarian slaves. "What will be left to us?" they asked. "Your lives", was the reply.

The pagan senators of Rome attributed the cruel disaster which had come upon them to the wrath of the gods at the abandonment of the old religion. The blockade, continued a few days longer, would force them to accept Alaric's cruel terms. The only hope lay in reconciling the angry deities, if perchance they might save the city. Encouraging news arrived at this moment that in the Umbrian town of Narnia, to which Alaric had laid siege on his march, sacrifices had been performed, and that miraculous fire and thunder had frightened the Goths into abandoning the siege. The general opinion was that the same means should be tried at Rome. The prefect of the city, Pompeianus, thought it well that the Christians should share in the responsibility for such a violation of the laws, and he laid the matter before the Pope, Innocent I. The Pope is said to have "considered the safety of the city more important than his own opinion", and to have consented to the secret performance of the necessary rites. But the priests said that the rites would not avail unless they were celebrated publicly on the Capitol in the presence of the Senate, and in the Forum. Then the half-heartedness of the Roman pagans of that day was revealed. No one could be found with the courage to perform the ceremonies in public.

After this futile interlude, nothing remained but, in a chastened and humble spirit, to send another embassy to Alaric and seek to move his compassion. After prolonged negotiations he granted tolerable terms. He would depart, without entering the city, on receiving 5000 pounds of gold (about £225,000), 30,000 of silver, 4000 silk tunics, 3000 scarlet-dyed skins, and 3000 pounds of pepper, and the Senate was to bring pressure to bear on the Emperor to conclude peace and alliance with the Goths. As the treasury was empty, and the contributions of the citizens fell short of the required amount of gold and silver, the ornaments were stripped from the images of the gods and some gold and silver statues were melted down to make up the ransom of the city. Before delivering the treasure to Alaric, messengers were despatched to Ravenna to obtain the Emperor's sanction of the terms, and his promise to hand over to Alaric some noble hostages and conclude a peace. Honorius agreed, and Alaric duly received the treasures of Rome. He then withdrew his army to the southern borders of Etruria to await the fulfilment of the Emperor's promise (December A.D. 408). The number of his followers was soon increased by the flight from Rome of a multitude of the barbarian slaves whose surrender he had formerly demanded. They flocked to his camp, and it is said that his host, thus reinforced, was 40,000 strong.

At a conference which was held with one of the imperial ministers at Ariminum he asked for the provinces of Noricum, Venetia, Istria, and Dalmatia. This was a large demand. The cession of Venetia was out of the question. It would have placed the peninsula at the mercy of the Visigoths. They would have held the gates. Alaric can hardly have hoped that his whole demand would be granted. Negotiations were broken off, but presently he reduced his extravagant demand to the province of Noricum. He also required an annual supply of food, and a Roman official dignity which meant a Mastership of Soldiers. In the circumstances it would have been wise of the government of Honorius to yield; but they now felt themselves stronger; they had been gathering new forces, and Alaric's multitudes were probably in difficulties about their food supply. Hence the terms were refused.

Alaric then marched on Rome for the second time towards the end of 409, and forced the Senate to elect a rival Emperor, Priscus Attalus, who he hoped would be more obedient to him than Honorius. But he did not find Attalus a pliant tool, and after some months he entered into negotiations with Honorius. He could now approach the Emperor with a good chance, as he thought, of concluding a satisfactory settlement. Leaving his main army at Ariminum, he had a personal interview with Honorius a few miles from Ravenna (July A.D. 410). At this juncture the Visigoth Sarus appeared upon the scene and changed the course of history. He had been a rival of Alaric and a friend of Stilicho, and had deserted his people to enter the Roman service. Hitherto he had taken no part in the struggle between the Romans and his own nation, but had maintained a watching attitude in Picenum, where he was stationed with three hundred followers. He now declared himself for Honorius, and he resolved to prevent the conclusion of peace. His motives are not clear, but, whatever they were, he attacked Alaric's camp. Alaric suspected that he had acted not without the Emperor's knowledge, and, enraged at such a flagrant violation of the truce, he broke off the negotiations, and marched upon Rome for the third time.

Having surrounded the city and once more reduced the inhabitants to the verge of starvation, he effected an entry at night through the Salarian Gate – doubtless by the assistance of traitors from within – on August 24, A.D. 410. This time the Gothic king was in no humour to spare the capital of the world. He allowed his followers to slay, burn, and pillage at will. The sack lasted for two or three days. It is true that some respect was shown for churches; and stories were told to show that the violence of the rapacious Goths was mitigated by veneration for Christian institutions. There is no reason to suppose that all the buildings and antiquities of the city suffered extensive damage. The palace of Sallust, in the north of the city, was burnt down, and excavations on the Aventine, in the fifth century a fashionable aristocratic quarter, have revealed many traces of the fires with which the barbarians destroyed the houses they had plundered. A rich booty and numerous captives, among whom was the Emperor's sister, Galla Placidia, were taken.

DEATH OF ALARIC

On the third day Alaric led his triumphant host forth from the humiliated city, which it had been his fortune to devastate with fire and sword. He marched southward through Campania, took Nola and Capua, but failed to capture Naples. He did not tarry over the siege of this city, for his object was to cross over to Africa, probably for the purpose of establishing himself and his people in that rich country. Throughout their movements in Italy, the food supply had been a vital question for the Goths; and to seize Africa, the granary of Italy, whether for its own sake, or as a step to seizing Italy itself, was an obvious course. The Gothic host reached Rhegium; ships were gathered to transport it to Messina, but a storm suddenly arose and wrecked them in the straits. Without ships, Alaric was forced to retire on his footsteps, perhaps hoping to collect a fleet at Naples. But his days were numbered. He died at Consentia (Cosenza) before the end of the year (A.D. 410); his followers buried him in the Basentus, and diverted its waters into another channel, that his body might never be desecrated. It is related that the men who were employed on the work were all massacred, that the secret might not be divulged.

The interest of Alaric's career perhaps consists in this: he belongs to the same class of leaders as those forgotten chieftains who led the Goths from the shores of the Baltic to the shores of the Euxine, and then to Dacia. The migration which he heads is through the provinces of the Empire; we can follow his folk and their wagons, in the full light of day; and the anomaly of seeing within the lands of civilisation a movement such as we associate with the wilds and forests of Central Europe has lent a particular fascination to the career of Alaric. He was a Christian, he had held office in the imperial service; but we feel that he ought to have been a pagan, and that he was unsuited for posts in the Roman army. He was more competent perhaps to lead a migration than to found a settlement; and he was unequal to coping with the circumstances in which he was placed, though they were exceptionally favourable. He belonged in temper and capacity to an older order of things; he was born out of his due time; but though he failed in his undertaking, he drew upon himself the regard of the whole world.

ATAULF AND GALLA PLACIDA

In his Italian expedition Alaric had been assisted and supported by his brother-in-law, Ataulf. The Goths elected him their king on Alaric's death, and on him it devolved to find an expedient to deliver his fold from the *impasse* into which Alaric had led them. The new king was different from the old in character and ideas. He at first had less reverence for Roman civilisation than Alaric; he was more devoted to the ways and manners of his own people. But he changed. We are fortunate enough to possess a remarkable testimony as to his ideals. It is preserved by Orosius, a Spaniard, who was a contemporary and who completed his work *Against the Pagans* about 418; and Orosius derived it directly from a citizen of Narbo Martius who had been on terms of intimacy with the Gothic king. This person heard Ataulf say that at one time he had aspired to abolish the Roman name, to turn Romania into Gothia, to make himself a Gothic Emperor. But experience taught him that the Goths were by themselves too lawless and unteachable to be the successors of the Romans, and so he changed his mind: he formed the idea of using Gothic vigour to restore the Roman name, and of being handed down to posterity as the *restitutor orbis Romani*. Thus from having been anti-Roman *à outrance*, and cherishing dreams which would not have tempted even Alaric, Ataulf became a convert to Rome.

Of his doings in Italy during the thirteen or fourteen months which elapsed between Alaric's death and the entry of Ataulf into Gaul we hear almost nothing. It is hardly probable that he visited Rome and plundered it again; but Etruria was laid waste by him.

Ataulf crossed the Alps early in A.D. 412, perhaps by the pass of Mont Genèvre, to play a leading part in the troubled politics of Gaul, taking with him his captive Galla Placidia and the deposed Emperor Attalus. The Goths were then involved for some time in hostile operations against a pretender named Jovinus in south-eastern Gaul; here they acted successfully in support of Honorius, and for a moment the authority of that Emperor was supreme in Gaul.

Ataulf then moved westward and established himself in Narbonensis and Aquitania. He took Narbonne, Toulouse, and Bordeaux, and determined to give himself a new status by allying himself in marriage to the Theodosian house. Negotiations with Ravenna were doubtless carried on during his military operations, but he now persuaded Placidia, against the will of her brother, to give him her hand. The nuptials were celebrated in Roman form (in January, A.D. 414) at Narbonne, in the house of a leading citizen. We are told that, arrayed in Roman dress, Placidia sat in the place of honour, the Gothic king at her side, he too dressed as a Roman. We know all too little of the personality of this lady, who was to play a considerable part in history for thirty years. She was now perhaps in her twenty-sixth year, but she may have been younger. Her personal attractiveness is shown by the passion she inspired in Constantius, and the strength of her character by various incidents of her life – such as her defiance of her brother's wishes in uniting herself to the Goth – in which she displayed marked independence. She was in later years to become the ruler of the west.

The friendly advances which were now made to Honorius by the barbarian who had forced himself upon him as a brother-in-law were rejected. Ataulf then resorted to the policy of Alaric. He caused the old tyrant Attalus to be again invested with the purple. Constantius, the Master of Soldiers, went forth for a second time to Arles to suppress the usurper and settle accounts with the Goths. He prevented all ships from reaching the coast of Septimania, as the territory of Narbonensis was now commonly called. The Goths were thus deprived of the provisions which reached Narbonne by sea, and their position became difficult. Ataulf led them southward to Barcelona, probably hoping to establish himself in Tarraconensis (early in A.D. 415). But before they left Gaul, the Goths laid waste southern Aquitania and set Bordeaux on fire. Attalus was left behind and abandoned to his fate, as he was no longer of any use to the Goths. Indeed his elevation had been a mistake. He had no adherents in Gaul, no money, no army, no one to support him except the barbarians themselves. He escaped from Gaul in a ship, but was captured and delivered alive to Constantius.

At Barcelona a son was born to Ataulf and Placidia. They named him Theodosius after his grandfather, and the philo-Roman feelings of Ataulf were confirmed. The death of the child soon after birth was a heavy blow: the body was buried, in a silver coffin, near the city. Ataulf did not long survive him. He was slain by the private vengeance of a servant (September A.D. 415).

WALLIA AND THE SETTLEMENT IN GAUL

After a short intervening reign Wallia was elected king; and Wallia is an important person in the history of the Visigoths, for it was he who succeeded in marking out the limits of their new kingdom in Gaul.

But in order to understand the position of Wallia and his people we must retrace nearly ten years and follow the fortunes of that torrent of barbarians which had poured into Gaul at the end of the year A.D. 406. You remember the names of the four peoples which participated in the invasion: the two Vandal peoples, the Asdings and the Silings, and their allies, the Sueves and the Alans. Crossing the Rhine near the point where the Main joins it, their first exploit was to plunder Mayence and massacre many of the inhabitants, who had sought refuge in a church. Then advancing through Germania Prima they entered Belgica, and following the road to Treves they sacked and set fire to that imperial city. Still continuing their westward path, they crossed the Meuse and the Aisne, and wrought their will on Reims. From here they seem to have turned northward. Amiens, Arras, and Tournay were their prey: they reached Terouanne, not far from the sea, due east of Boulogne, but Boulogne itself they did not venture to attack. After this diversion to the north, they pursued their course of devastation southward, crossing the Seine and the Loire into Aquitania, up to the foot of the Pyrenees. Few towns could resist them. Toulouse was one of the few, and its successful defence is said to have been due to the energy of its bishop Exuperius.

Such, so far as we can conjecture from the evidence of our meagre sources, was the general course of this invasion, but we may be sure that the barbarians broke up into several hosts and followed a wide track, dividing among them the joys of plunder and destruction. Pious verse-writers of the time, who witnessed this visitation, painted the miseries of the helpless provinces vaguely and rhetorically, but perhaps truthfully enough, in order to point a moral:

uno fumavit Gallia tota rogo .

The terror of fire and sword was followed by the horror of hunger in a wasted land.

In eastern Gaul, too, some famous cities suffered grievously from German foes. But the calamities of Strassburg, Speier, and Worms were perhaps not the work of the Vandals and their associates. The Burgundians seem to have taken advantage of the crisis to push down the Main, and at the expense of the Alamanni to have occupied new territory astride the Rhine. And it is probably these two peoples, especially the Alamanni dislodged from their homes, who were responsible for the havoc wrought in the province of Upper Germany.

The barbarians remained in Gaul for more than two years; then in 409 they crossed the Pyrenees and inundated Spain. I ought to observe that the Vandals, like the Visigoths, were Christians, of the Arian creed. They had embraced this religion while they lived on Roman soil in Pannonia, and, as their dialect seems to have been very close to that of the Goths, they were able to use the scriptures of Wulfilas. It is interesting to find it mentioned that they carried with them to Spain the *Liber divinae legis* and consulted it as an oracle.

Accordingly, when Ataulf led his Goths to the confines of Gaul and Spain, he found Spain overrun by barbarian strangers of whom some, viz. the Vandals, were closely akin to his own people. Thus in Spain and the immediately adjacent regions of Gaul there were (A.D. 413-415) no less than five politically distinct peoples – the Asding Vandals, the Siling Vandals, the Sueves, the Alans, and the Visigoths themselves – seeking to form settlements.

In A.D. 415, when on Ataulf's death Wallia came to the throne, the idea of the Goths seems to have been to occupy the eastern provinces of Spain. But there they found themselves met by the same difficulty which they had to face in Italy, viz. want of food. The land had been overrun by the other barbarians, and the Roman fleet blockaded the ports. Hereupon Wallia resumed Alaric's idea, to cross over to Africa and take possession of the Roman granary. His project met a similar fate. Ships which he sent in advance to the opposite coast were destroyed by a storm, and, whether from superstitious fear or from want of transports, he relinquished his idea, and was perforce compelled to make terms with Constantius, who was near to the Pyrenees. He received a large supply of corn, and in return Galla Placidia, Ataulf's queen, who was still with the Goths, was restored to her brother Honorius. Wallia also undertook to render military service to the Empire by clearing Spain of the other barbarians.

These other barbarians had first of all devastated Spain far and wide, and had then settled down, with the intention of occupying permanently the various provinces. The Siling Vandals, under their king Fredbal, took Baetica in the south; the Alans, under their king Addac, made their abode in Lusitania, which corresponds roughly to Portugal; the Suevians, and the Asding Vandals, whose king was Gunderic, occupied the north-western province of Gallaecia north of the Douro. The eastern provinces of Tarraconensis and Carthaginiensis, though the western portions may have been seized, and though they were doubtless constantly harried by raids, did not pass under the power of the invaders.

Wallia began operations by attacking the Silings in Baetica. Before the end of the year he had captured their king by a ruse and sent him to the Emperor. The intruders in Spain were alarmed, and their one thought was to make peace with Honorius, and obtain by formal grant the lands which they had taken by violence. They all sent embassies to Ravenna. The obvious policy of the imperial government was to sow jealousy and hostility among them by receiving favourably the proposals of some and rejecting those of others. The Asdings and the Suevians appear to have been successful in obtaining the recognition of Honorius as federates, while the Silings and Alans were told that their presence on Roman soil would not be tolerated. Their subjugation by Wallia was a task of about two years. The Silings would not yield, and they were virtually exterminated. The king of the Alans was slain, and the remnant of the people who escaped the sword of the Goths fled to Gallaecia and attached themselves to the fortunes of the Asding Vandals. Gunderic thus became "King of the Vandals and Alans", and the title was always retained by his successors.

After these successful campaigns the Visigoths were recompensed by receiving a permanent home. The imperial government decided that they should be settled in a Gallic, not a Spanish, province, and Constantius recalled Wallia from Spain to Gaul. A compact was made by which the whole rich province of Aquitania Secunda, extending from the Garonne to the Loire, with parts of the adjoining provinces (Narbonensis and Novempopulana), were granted to the Goths. The two great cities on the banks of the Garonne, Bordeaux and Toulouse, were handed over to Wallia. But Narbonne and the Mediterranean coast were reserved for the Empire. As federates, the Goths had no authority over the Roman provincials, who remained under the control of the imperial administration. And the Roman proprietors retained one-third of their lands; two-thirds were resigned to the Goths. Thus, from the point of view of the Empire, south-western Gaul remained an integral part of the realm; part of the land passed into the possession of federates who acknowledged the authority of Honorius; the provincials obeyed, as before, the Emperor's laws and were governed by the Emperor's officials. From the Gothic point of view, a Gothic kingdom had been established in Aquitania, for the moment confined by restraints which it would be the task of the Goths to break through, and limited territorially by boundaries which it would be their policy to overpass. Not that at this time, or for long after, they thought of renouncing their relation to the Empire as federates, but they were soon to show that they would seize any favourable opportunity to increase their power and extend their borders.

Lecture 7:
Gaul, Spain, and Africa in Transition

THE VISIGOTHIC KINGDOM OF TOULOUSE – SUEVES AND VANDALS IN SPAIN – GALLA PLACIDIA AND BONIFACE – THE VANDAL CONQUEST OF AFRICA – AETIUS AND VALENTINIAN III.

The Visigoths had now obtained a permanent home by the shores of the Atlantic. This final settlement of the Visigoths, who had moved about for twenty years in the three peninsulas of the Mediterranean, was a momentous stage in that process of compromise between the Roman Empire and the Germans which had been going on for many years and was ultimately to change the whole face of western Europe. Constantius was doing in Gaul what Theodosius the Great had done in the Balkans. There were now two orderly Teutonic kingdoms on Gallic soil under Roman lordship, the Burgundian on the Rhine, the Visigothic on the Atlantic.

Wallia did not live to see the arrangements which he had made for his people carried into effect. He died a few months after the conclusion of the compact, and a grandson of Alaric was elected to the throne, Theodoric I. (A.D. 418). Upon him it devolved to superintend the partition of the lands which the Roman proprietors were obliged to surrender to the Goths. It must have taken a considerable time to complete the transfer. The Visigoths received the lion's share. Each landlord retained one-third of his property for himself and handed over the remaining portion to one of the German strangers. This arrangement was more unfavourable to the Empire than arrangements of the same kind which were afterwards made in Gaul and in Italy with other intruders (as we shall see in due course). For in these other cases it was the Germans who received the third, the Romans retaining the larger share. And this was the normal proportion. For the principle of these arrangements was directly derived from the old Roman system of quartering soldiers on the owners of land. On that system, which dated from the days of the Republic, and was known as *hospitalitas* , the owner was bound to give one-third of the produce of his property to the guests whom he reluctantly harboured. This principle was now applied to the land itself, and the same term was used; the proprietors and the barbarians with whom they were compelled to share their estate were designated as host and guest (*hospites*).

This fact illustrates the gradual nature of the process by which western Europe passed from the power of the Roman into that of the Teuton. Transactions which virtually meant the surrender of provinces to invaders were, in their immediate aspect, merely the application of an old Roman principle, adapted indeed to changed conditions. Thus the process of the dismemberment of the Empire was eased; the transition to an entirely new order of things was masked; a system of federate states within the Empire prepared the way for the system of independent states which was to replace the Empire. The change was not accomplished without much violence and even continuous warfare; but it was not cataclysmic.

The problem which faced the imperial government in Gaul was much larger than the mere settlement of the Gothic nation in Aquitania. The whole country required reorganisation, if the imperial authority was to be maintained effectively as of old in the provinces. The events of the last ten years – the ravages of the barbarians, and the wars with the tyrants – had disorganised the whole administrative system. The lands north of the Loire – Armorica in the large sense of the name – had in the days of the tyrant Constantine been practically independent, and it was the work of Exuperantius to restore some semblance of law and order in these provinces. Most of the great cities in the south and east had been sacked, or burned, or besieged. We saw how imperial Treves, the seat of the praetorian prefect, had been captured and plundered by the Vandals: since then it had been, twice at least, devastated by the Franks with sword and fire. The Prefect of the Gauls translated his residence from the Moselle to the Rhone, and Arles succeeded to the dignity of Treves.

What Constantius and his advisers did for the restoration of northern Gaul is unknown, but the direction of their policy is probably indicated by the measure which they adopted in the south, in the diocese of Septimania. On April 17, A.D. 418, Honorius issued an edict enacting that a representative assembly was to meet every autumn at Arles, to debate questions of public interest. It was to consist of (1) the seven governors of the seven provinces, of (2) the highest class of the decurions, and of (3) representatives of the landed proprietors. The council had no independent powers; its object was to make common suggestions for the removal of abuses or for improvements in administration, on which the praetorian prefect might act himself or make representations to the central government. Or it might concert measures for common action in such matters as a petition to the Emperor or the prosecution of a corrupt official.

Such a council was not a new experiment. The old provincial assemblies of the early Empire had generally fallen into disuse in the third century, but in the fourth we find provincial assemblies in Africa, and diocesan assemblies in Africa and possibly in Spain. Already in the reign of Honorius, a praetorian prefect, Petronius, had made an attempt to create a diocesan assembly in southern Gaul, probably in the hope that time and labour might be saved if the affairs of the various provinces were all brought before him in the same month of the year. The Edict of A.D. 418 was a revival of this idea, but had a wider scope and intention. It was expressly urged that the object of the assembly was not merely to debate public questions, but also to promote social intercourse and trade. The advantages of Arles – a favourite city of Constantine the Great, on which he had bestowed a name based on his own or that of his eldest son, Constantina – and its busy commercial life are thus described in the Edict: "All the famous products of the rich Orient, of perfumed Arabia and delicate Assyria, of fertile Africa, fair Spain, and brave Gaul, abound here so profusely that one might think the various marvels of the world were indigenous in its soil. Built at the junction of the Rhone with the Tuscan sea, it unites all the enjoyments of life and all the facilities of trade."

It must also have been present to the mind of Constantius that the Assembly, attracting every year to Arles a considerable number of the richest and most notable people from Aquitania Secunda and Novempopulana, would enable the provincials, surrounded by Visigothic neighbours, to keep in touch with the rest of the Empire, and would help to counteract the influence which would inevitably be brought to bear upon them from the barbarian court of Toulouse.

SUEVES AND VANDALS IN SPAIN

The prospect of a return to peace and settled life in Spain seemed more distant than in Gaul. Soon after the Visigoths had departed, war broke out between Gunderic, king of the Asding Vandals, and Hermeric, king of the Suevians. The latter were blockaded in the Nervasian mountains, but suddenly Asterius, Count of the Spains, appeared upon the scene, and his operations compelled the Vandals to abandon the blockade: at Bracara a large number were slain by the Roman forces. Then the Vandals and Alans, who now formed one nation, left Gallaecia and migrated to Baetica. On their way they met the Master of Soldiers, Castinus, who had come from Italy to restore order in the peninsula. He had a large army, including a force of Visigothic federates, but he suffered a severe defeat, partly through the perfidious conduct of his Gothic allies. The Vandals established themselves in Baetica, but it does not appear whether the recognition they had received in Gallaecia as a federate people was renewed when they took up their abode in the southern province (A.D. 422).

GALLA PLACIDIA AND BONIFACE

We have now reached what may be considered the end of the first stage in the process of the dismemberment of the Roman Empire and the establishment of German kingdoms in the west – about the year 423, the year in which the Emperor Honorius died. At this time there were three German kingdoms in Gaul, dependent on the Empire – federate kingdoms, viz. (1) That of the Visigoths in south-western Gaul. (2) That of the Burgundians towards the south-east. (3) The older federate dependency of the Salian Franks in the north-east on the lower Rhine.

In Spain there were two, viz.: (1) the Suevians in the north-west – Gallaecia. (2) The Vandals, in whom the Alans had been merged, in the south, in Baetica. Three of these five were East Germans; the Visigoths, Burgundians, and Vandals. Two were West Germans; the Salians and Sueves.

In what we may call the second period of the process of dismemberment, in which the Empire had to defend itself against the hostilities and covetousness of all these German dependencies, it was the Vandals, who had now established themselves at the western sea gate of the Mediterranean, who played the most prominent part and most seriously affected the fortunes of Rome.

Africa – far from the Rhine and Danube, across which the great East German nations had been pouring into the Roman Empire – had not yet been violated by the feet of Teutonic foes. But the frustrated plans of Alaric and Wallia were intimations that the day might be at hand when this province too would have to meet the crisis of a German invasion. The third attempt was not to fail, but it was not the Goths to whom the granaries of Africa were to fall. The Vandal people, perhaps the first of the East German peoples to cross the Baltic, was destined to find its last home and its grave in this land so distant from its cradle.

We saw how the Vandals settled in Baetica, and how King Gunderic assumed the title of "King of the Vandals and the Alans". He conquered New Carthage and Hispalis (Seville), and made raids on the Balearic Islands and possibly on Mauretania Tingitana. He died in A.D. 428 and was succeeded by his brother Gaiseric, who had perhaps already shared the kingship with him. About the same time events in Africa opened a new and attractive prospect to the Vandals.

To understand the situation I must briefly explain what happened in Italy after the death of Honorius. Constantius, the great general who was supreme in conducting the government during the second half of the reign of Honorius, was, as we saw, responsible for settling the two federate kingdoms in Gaul – Visigoths and Burgundians – and also for settling Spain. He had married the Emperor's sister, Ataulf's widow, Galla Placidia, and had been afterwards crowned Augustus, and elevated to be the colleague of Honorius, but had died before he had been a year on the throne (421). When Honorius died two years later, Galla Placidia and her two infant children, a boy and a girl, were at Constantinople. The boy's name was Valentinian, the girl's Honoria. Valentinian was the natural claimant to the succession, as Honorius had had no children of his own. But meanwhile in Italy a certain civil servant, named John, was proclaimed Emperor, and it was necessary for Galla Placidia, supported by the armies of her nephew Theodosius II., who was reigning at Constantinople, to fight for the throne. John was defeated and executed, after which the child Valentinian was crowned Augustus at Rome towards the end of 425. Thus it came about that for some twelve years, *i.e.* so long as Valentinian III. was a minor (425-437), western Europe was governed by Galla Placidia (formerly queen of the Goths), as regent for her son.

Now during the struggle between the usurper John and Galla Placidia two military men had been prominent, and had taken opposite sides. One was Boniface, the other Aetius. Boniface had supported Placidia; while Aetius had enlisted a contingent of Huns to fight for John. The Huns arrived too late; John had already been captured; but Aetius was able to make terms with the regent and was given a command in Gaul, where he did good work in defending the south against the Goths and the north against encroachments of the Franks.

As for Boniface, who was the military commander in Africa, his conduct laid him open to the suspicion that he was aiming at a tyranny himself. It had been a notable part of his policy, since he assumed the military command in Africa, to exhibit deep devotion to the Church and to co-operate cordially with the bishops. He ingratiated himself with the famous Augustine, bishop of Hippo, and a letter of Augustine casts some welcome though dim light on the highly ambiguous behaviour of the count in these fateful years. Notwithstanding his professions of orthodox zeal, and hypocritical pretences that he longed to retire into monastic life, Boniface took as his second wife an Arian lady, and allowed his daughter to be baptised into the Arian communion. This apostasy shocked and grieved Augustine, but it was a more serious matter politically that, instead of devoting all his energies to repelling the incursions of the Moors, he was working to make his own authority absolute in Africa. So at least it seemed to the court of Ravenna, and Galla Placidia – doubtless by the advice of Felix, who had been appointed Master of Soldiers – recalled him to account for his conduct. Boniface refused to come, and placed himself in the position of an "enemy of the Republic". An army was immediately sent against him under three commanders, all of whom were slain (A.D. 427). Then at the beginning of A.D. 428 another army was sent under the command of Sigisvult, a Goth, who seems to have been named Count of Africa and commissioned to replace the rebel. Sigisvult appears to have succeeded in seizing Hippo and Carthage, and Boniface, despairing of overcoming him by his own forces, resorted to the plan of inviting the Vandals to come to his aid.

THE VANDAL CONQUEST OF AFRICA

The proposal of Boniface was to divide Africa between himself and the Vandal king, for whom he doubtless destined the three Mauretanian provinces; and he undertook to furnish the means of transport. Gaiseric accepted the invitation. He fully realised the value of the possession of Africa, which had attracted the ambition of two Gothic kings. The whole nation of the Vandals and Alans embarked in May A.D. 429, and crossed over to Africa. If the united peoples numbered, as is said, 80,000, the fighting force might have been about 15,000.

Their king Gaiseric stands out among the German leaders of his time as unquestionably the ablest. He had not only the military qualities which most of them possessed, but he was also master of a political craft which was rare among the German leaders of the migrations. His ability was so exceptional that his irregular birth – his mother was a slave – did not diminish his influence and prestige. We have a description of him, which seems to come from a good source. "Of medium height, lame from a fall of his horse, he had a deep mind and was sparing of speech. Luxury he despised, but his anger was uncontrollable and he was covetous. He was far-sighted in inducing foreign peoples to act in his interests, and resourceful in sowing seeds of discord and stirring up hatred." All that we know of his long career bears out this suggestion of astute and perfidious diplomacy.

The unhappy population of the Mauretanian regions were left unprotected to the mercies of the invaders, and, if we can trust the accounts that have come down to us, they seem to have endured horrors such as the German conquerors of this age seldom inflicted upon defenceless provinces. The Visigoths were lambs compared with the Vandal wolves. Neither age nor sex was spared, and cruel tortures were applied to force the victims to reveal suspected treasures. The bishops and clergy, the churches and sacred vessels, were not spared. We get a glimpse of the situation in the correspondence of St. Augustine. Bishops write to him to ask whether it is right to allow their flocks to flee from the approaching danger, and for themselves to abandon their sees. The invasion was a signal to other enemies, whether of Rome or of the Roman government, to join in the fray. The Moors were encouraged in their depredations, and religious heretics and sectaries, especially the Donatists, seized the opportunity to wreak vengeance on the society which oppressed them.

If Africa was to be saved, it was necessary that the Roman armies should be united, and Galla Placidia immediately took steps to regain the allegiance of Boniface. A reconciliation was effected by the good offices of a certain Darius, of illustrious rank, whom she sent to Africa, and he seems also to have concluded a truce with Gaiseric, which was, however, of but brief duration, for the Roman proposals were not accepted. Gaiseric was determined to pillage, if he could not conquer, the rich eastern provinces of Africa. He entered Numidia, defeated Boniface, and besieged him in Hippo (May to June A.D. 430). The city held out for more than a year. Then Gaiseric raised the siege (July A.D. 431). New forces were sent from Italy and Constantinople under the command of Aspar, the general of Theodosius; a battle was fought, and Aspar and Boniface were so utterly defeated that they could make no further effort to resist the invader. Hippo was taken soon afterwards, and the only important towns which held out were Carthage and Cirta.

AETIUS AND VALENTINIAN III

During the years 425-429, the right-hand minister of Galla Placidia, the Master of Both Services, was Felix. But Aetius by 429 had won such prestige by his successes in Gaul against the Goths and Franks (though Placidia had never forgiven him for his espousal of the cause of John) that he was able to impose his own terms, and extort from her the deposition of Felix and his own elevation to the post which Felix had occupied. He was appointed Master of Both Services in A.D. 429, and it is said that he at once caused Felix to be killed on suspicion of treachery. Then Boniface returned to Italy, where Placidia received him with favour, and soon afterwards she deposed the hated Aetius, who was consul of the year (A.D. 432), and gave his military command to the repentant rebel, on whom at the same time she conferred the dignity of patrician. Aetius refused to submit. There was civil war in Italy. The rivals fought a battle near Ariminum, in which Boniface was victorious, but he died shortly afterwards from a malady, perhaps caused by a wound. Aetius escaped to Dalmatia and journeyed to the court of his friend Rugila, the king of the Huns. By his help, we know not how, he was able to reappear in Italy, to dictate terms to the court of Ravenna, and obtain for himself reinstatement in his old office and elevation to the rank of patrician (A.D. 434).

In the meantime, during this obscure struggle for power, the Vandals were extending their conquests in Numidia. In spite of his wonderfully rapid career of success, Gaiseric was ready to come to terms with the Empire. Aetius, who was fully occupied in Gaul, where the Visigoths and Burgundians were actively aggressive, saw that the forces at his disposal were unequal to the expulsion of the Vandals, and thought that it was better to share Africa with the intruders than to lose it entirely. Gaiseric probably wished to consolidate his power in the provinces which he had occupied, and knew that any compact he might make would not be an obstacle to further conquests. Hippo, from which the inhabitants had fled, seems to have been reoccupied by the Romans, and here (February 11, A.D. 435) a treaty was concluded. The Vandals were to retain the provinces which they had occupied, viz. the two Mauretanias and a part of Numidia, but were to pay an annual tribute, thus acknowledging the overlordship of Rome.

Aetius had now firmly established his power, and Galla Placidia had to resign herself to his guidance. Valentinian was fifteen years of age, and the regency could not last much longer. The presence of the Master of Soldiers was soon demanded in Gaul, where the Visigoths were again bent on new conquests and where the Burgundians were invading the province of Upper Belgica (A.D. 435). Against the Burgundians he does not appear to have sent a Roman army; he asked his friends the Huns to chastise them. The Huns knew how to strike. It is said that 20,000 Burgundians were slain, and King Gundahar was one of those who fell (A.D. 436). Thus came to an end the first Burgundian kingdom in Gaul, with its royal residence at Worms. It was the background of the heroic legends which passed into the German epic – the Nibelungenlied. The Burgundians were not exterminated, and a few years later the Roman government assigned territory to the remnant of the nation in Sapaudia (Savoy) south of Lake Geneva (A.D. 443).

Narbonne was besieged by Theodoric, king of the Visigoths, in A.D. 436, but was relieved by Litorius, who was probably the Master of Soldiers in Gaul. Three years later the same commander drove the Goths back to the walls of their capital Toulouse, and it is interesting to find him gratifying his Hun soldiers by the performance of pagan rites and the consultation of the auspices. These ceremonies, however, did not help him. Fortune turned against him. He was defeated and taken prisoner in a battle outside the city. Avitus, the Praetorian Prefect of Gaul, who had great influence with Theodoric, then brought about the conclusion of peace. In these years there were also troubles in the provinces north of the Loire, where the Armoricans rebelled, and Aetius or his lieutenant Litorius was compelled to reimpose upon them the "liberty" of imperial rule.

In A.D. 437 Aetius was consul for the second time, and in that year Valentinian went to Constantinople to wed his affianced bride, Licinia Eudoxia the daughter of Theodosius. Now assuredly, if not before, the regency was at an end, and henceforward Aetius had to do in all high affairs not with Galla Placidia, who distrusted and disliked him, but with an inexperienced youth. Valentinian was weak and worthless. He had been spoiled by his mother, and had grown up to be a man of pleasure who took no serious interest in his imperial duties. He associated, we are told, with astrologers and sorcerers, and was constantly engaged in amours with other men's wives, though his own wife was exceptionally beautiful. He had some skill in riding and in archery and was a good runner, if we may believe Flavius Vegetius Renatus, who dedicated to him a treatise on the art of war.

From the end of the regency to his own death, Aetius was master of the Empire in the west, and it must be imputed to his policy and arms that imperial rule did not break down in all the provinces by the middle of the fifth century. Of his work during these critical years we have no history. We know little more than what we can infer from some bald notices in chronicles written by men who selected their facts without much discrimination. If we possessed the works of the court poet of the time we might know more, for even from the few fragments which have survived we learn facts unrecorded elsewhere. The Spaniard, Flavius Merobaudes, did for Valentinian and Aetius what Claudian had done for Honorius and Stilicho, though with vastly inferior talent.

The position of Aetius in these years as the supreme minister was confirmed by the betrothal of his son to the Emperor's daughter Placidia, an arrangement which can hardly have been welcome to Galla Placidia, the Augusta. With Valentinian himself he can hardly have been on intimate terms. The fact that he had supported the tyrant John was probably never forgiven. And it cannot have been agreeable to the young Emperor that it was found necessary to curtail his income and rob his privy purse in order to help the state in its financial straits. Little revenue could come from Africa, suffering from the ravages of the Vandals, and in A.D. 439, as we shall see, the richest provinces of that country passed into the hands of the barbarians. The income derived from Gaul, too, must have been very considerably reduced, and we are not surprised to find the government openly acknowledging in A.D. 444 that "the strength of our treasury is unable to meet the necessary expenses".

Meanwhile the treaty of A.D. 435 was soon violated by Gaiseric. He did not intend to stop short of the complete conquest of Roman Africa. In less than five years Carthage was taken (October 19, A.D. 439). If there was any news that could shock or terrify men who remembered that twenty-nine years before Rome herself had been in the hands of the Goths, it was the news that an enemy was in possession of the city which in long past ages had been her most formidable rival. Italy trembled; for with a foe master of Carthage she felt that her own shores and cities were no longer safe. And, in fact, not many months passed before it was known that Gaiseric had a large fleet prepared to sail, although its destination was unknown. Rome and Naples were put into a state of defence; Sigisvult, Master of Soldiers, took steps to guard the coasts; Aetius and his army were summoned from Gaul; and the Emperor Theodosius prepared to send help. There was indeed some reason for alarm at Constantinople. The Vandal pirates could afflict the eastern as well as the western coasts of the Mediterranean; the security of commerce was threatened. It was even thought advisable to fortify the shores and harbours of the Bosphorus. The Mediterranean was no longer a Roman lake.

Lecture 8:
A New Menace to the Empire

THE TREATY BETWEEN AETIUS AND GAISERIC – THE ANGLO-SAXON CONQUEST OF BRITAIN – THE HUNS AND ATTILA

THE TREATY BETWEEN AETIUS AND GAISERIC

One of the most notable achievements of Gaiseric was the creation of a sea-power rival to that of Rome. Nor, after its creation, did the Empire long have to await attack. In the year A.D. 440, informed of the active preparations for defence which were being made for the protection of the Italian coasts, Gaiseric directed his first sea attack against Sicily and laid siege to Palermo. This city, however, successfully defied him. Meanwhile a large fleet had been got ready at Constantinople, and in. 441 it sailed for the west with the purpose of blockading Carthage. It appeared in Sicilian waters, and Gaiseric, who had already abandoned his enterprise in Sicily and returned to Africa, was alarmed. He opened negotiations with Rome, and in the next year, 442, a new treaty was concluded. By this treaty Africa was divided anew between the two powers. The division reversed that of 435 and was far more disadvantageous to Rome. The Empire took back the two Mauretanian provinces, and ceded to the Vandals the Proconsular Province, including Carthage, the province of Byzacena (which lay farther east, between the Proconsular Province and Tripoli), and the greater part of Numidia. The most fertile and important portions of the African diocese of Tripoli remained to the Empire.

At the same time, seeing the struggle of the Vandals, and conscious of the growing decline of the imperial power in western Europe, where it was becoming increasingly difficult to defend Roman territory against the numerous enemies who in the shape of *federates* were continually trying to enlarge their own borders, Aetius, in whose hands were now centred the government and policy of the west, decided that the best policy was to cultivate friendly relations with Gaiseric, who was much the ablest of his opponents, and to avoid giving that ambitious monarch any pretext for attacking Sicily again, or Sardinia, or Italy itself; so he prevailed upon Valentinian to consent to a betrothal between his elder daughter Eudocia and Gaiseric's son Huneric. It is probable that this arrangement was discussed at the time of the treaty, though it may not then have been definitely decided. But Huneric was already married. The Visigothic king Theodoric had bestowed upon him his daughter's hand. Such an alliance between Vandals and Goths could not have been welcome to Aetius; it was far more in the interest of his policy to keep alive between these two peoples the hostility which seems to have dated from the campaigns of Wallia in Spain. The existence of the Gothic wife was no hindrance to Gaiseric, and a pretext for repudiating her was easily found. She was accused of having plotted to poison him. She was punished by the mutilation of her ears and nose, and in this plight she was sent back to her father. The incident meant undying enmity between Visigoth and Vandal. Huneric, however, was free to contract a more dazzling matrimonial alliance with an imperial princess.

THE ANGLO-SAXON CONQUEST OF BRITAIN

In the meantime, while Africa was being lost, Aetius was busily engaged in defending Gaul against the encroachments of the Salian Franks in the north, and the Visigoths and Burgundians in the south. We will not consider the position of the Salian Franks till a later stage; nor need we go into the meagre details we have of the hostilities between Aetius and Theodoric I., the Visigothic king, for they did not lead to any noteworthy changes in the geography of Gaul. It must be imputed to the policy and ability of Aetius that imperial rule did not break down in all the provinces by the middle of the fifth century.

It had broken down in the extreme south in Africa; and it had also broken down in the extreme north, viz. in Britain; and the definite loss of these provinces should in my opinion be assigned towards about the same time. The year A.D. 442 is the date of the virtual loss of Africa, for though the Mauretanian provinces remained imperial for more than another decade, the best part of Africa was resigned. The date usually given for the abandonment of Britain is 410, but there is evidence which shows that Roman regiments and Roman officials were in the Britannic provinces as late as 430. Now according to the native British tradition the Anglo-Saxon occupation began about 428, whereas the Anglo-Saxon tradition which we find in Bede places the beginning of their dominion in 448. But in the contemporary Gallic Chronicle we get another date, *i.e.* 442, and I believe that this is the right one for the withdrawal of the Roman administration and the definite establishment of the Saxon power in the island.

During all these years, from the middle of the reign of Honorius to the middle of the century, Britain was suffering from constant raids not only of Saxons but also of Picts and Scots, and the natives of the south were taking flight from the island to the opposite coasts of Gaul or Armorica. This was the origin of Brittany.

The difficulties which beset Aetius in defending the western provinces were very grave, and were largely of a financial kind; they prevented him from taking active military measures against the Vandals; they compelled him to abandon the defence of Britain and to leave it to its enemies. But, apart from financial difficulties, a great and alarming change in the conditions of Europe had occurred about the year 435. From that year to 454 the European situation was dominated by the power and policy of the Huns.

THE HUNS AND ATTILA

Hitherto Aetius had been greatly aided in waging war against the Germans by the assistance of the Huns. He was a friend of the Hunnic king, Rugila, and we have seen how Rugila helped him in 433 by subduing the Burgundians. Now the tribes of the Huns were ruled each by its own chieftain, but Rugila seems to have brought together all the tribes into a sort of political unity. He had established himself between the Theiss and the Danube. The treaty which the government of Ravenna made with Rugila, when the Huns withdrew from Italy in A.D. 425 after the subjugation of the tyrant John, seems to have included the provision that the Huns should evacuate the Pannonian province of Valeria which they had occupied for forty-five years. But soon afterwards a new arrangement was made by which another part of Pannonia – apparently a district on the lower Save, but not including Sirmium – was surrendered to them. We may conjecture that this concession was made by Aetius in return for Rugila's help in A.D. 433.

Rugila died soon after the Burgundian war and he was succeeded by his nephews Bleda and Attila, the sons of Mundzuk, as joint rulers. Bleda played no part on the stage of history. Attila was a leading actor for twenty years, and his name is still almost a household word. He was not well favoured. His features, according to a Gothic historian, "bore the stamp of his origin; and the portrait of Attila exhibited the genuine deformity of a modern Kalmuck; a large head, a swarthy complexion, small deep-seated eyes, a flat nose, a few hairs in the place of a beard, broad shoulders, and a short square body of nervous strength though of a disproportioned form. The haughty step and demeanour of the king of the Huns expressed the consciousness of his superiority above the rest of mankind, and he had the custom of fiercely rolling his eyes as if he wished to enjoy the terror which he inspired".

Of Attila himself we have, indeed, a clearer impression than of any of the German kings who played leading parts in the period of the Wandering of the Nations. The historian Priscus, who accompanied his friend Maximin, the ambassador to Attila, in A.D. 448, and wrote a full account of the embassy, drew a vivid portrait of the monarch and described his court. The story is so interesting that I will reproduce some extracts from it:

"We set out with the barbarians, and arrived at Sardica, which is thirteen days for a fast traveller from Constantinople. Halting there we considered it advisable to invite Edecon and the barbarians with him to dinner. The inhabitants of the place sold us sheep and oxen, which we slaughtered, and we prepared a meal. In the course of the feast, as the barbarians lauded Attila and we lauded the Emperor, Bigilas remarked that it was not fair to compare a man and a god, meaning Attila by the man and Theodosius by the god. The Huns grew excited and hot at this remark. But we turned the conversation in another direction, and soothed their wounded feelings; and after dinner, when we separated, Maximin presented Edecon and Orestes with silk garments and Indian gems... . When we arrived at Naissus we found the city deserted, as though it had been sacked; only a few sick persons lay in the Churches. We halted at a short distance from the river, in an open space, for all the ground adjacent to the bank was full of the bones of men slain in war. On the morrow we came to the station of Agintheus, the commander-in-chief of the Illyrian armies (*magister militum per Illyricum*), who was posted not far from Naissus, to announce to him the imperial commands, and to receive five of those seventeen deserters, about whom Attila had written to the Emperor. We had an interview with him, and having treated the deserters with kindness, he committed them to us. The next day we proceeded from the district of Naissus towards the Danube. We entered a covered valley with many bends and windings and circuitous paths. We thought we were travelling due west, but when the day dawned the sun rose in front; and some of us unacquainted with the topography cried out that the sun was going the wrong way, and portending unusual events. The fact was that that part of the road faced the east, owing to the irregularity of the ground. Having passed these rough places we arrived at a plain which was also well wooded. At the river we were received by barbarian ferrymen, who rowed us across the river in boats made by themselves out of single trees hewn and hollowed. These preparations had not been made for our sake, but to convey across a company of Huns; for Attila pretended that he wished to hunt in Roman territory, but his intent was really hostile, because all the deserters had not been given up to him. Having crossed the Danube, and proceeded with the barbarians about seventy stadia, we were compelled to wait in a certain plain, that Edecon and his party might go on in front and inform Attila of our arrival. As we were dining in the evening we heard the sound of horses approaching, and two Scythians arrived with directions that we were to set out to Attila. We asked them first to partake of our meal, and they dismounted and made good cheer. On the next day, under their guidance, we arrived at the tents of Attila, which were numerous, about three o'clock, and when we wished to pitch our tent on a hill the barbarians who met us prevented us, because the tent of Attila was on low ground, so we halted where the Scythians desired... ." (Then a message is received from Attila, who was aware of the nature of their embassy, saying that if they had nothing further to communicate to him he would not receive them, so they reluctantly prepared to return.) "When the baggage had been packed on the beasts of burden, and we were perforce preparing to start in the night time, messengers came from Attila bidding us wait on account of the late hour. Then men arrived with an ox and river fish, sent to us by Attila, and when we had dined we retired to sleep. When it was day we expected a gentle and courteous message from the barbarian, but he again bade us depart if we had no further mandates beyond what he already knew. We made no reply, and prepared to set out, though Bigilas insisted that we should feign to have some other communication to make. When I saw that Maximin was very dejected, I went to Scottas (one of the Hun nobles, brother of Onegesius), taking with me Eusticius, who understood the Hun language. He had come with us to Scythia, not as a member of the embassy, but on business with Constantius, an Italian whom Aetius had sent to Attila to be that monarch's private secretary. I informed Scottas, Busticius acting as interpreter, that Maximin would give him many presents if he would procure him an interview with Attila; and, moreover, that the embassy would not only conduce to the public interests of the two powers, but to the private interest of Onegesius, for the Emperor desired that he should be sent as an ambassador to Byzantium, to arrange the disputes of the Huns and Romans, and that there he would receive splendid gifts. As Onegesius was not present it was for Scottas, I said, to help us, or rather help his brother, and at the same time prove that the report was true which ascribed to him an influence with Attila equal to that possessed by his brother. Scottas mounted his horse and rode to Attila's tent, while I returned to Maximin, and found him in a state of perplexity and anxiety, lying on the grass with Bigilas. I described my interview with Scottas, and bade him make preparations for an audience of Attila. They both jumped up, approving of what I had done, and recalled the men who had started with the beasts of burden. As we were considering what to say to Attila, and how to present the Emperor's gifts, Scottas came to fetch us, and we entered Attila's tent, which was surrounded by a multitude of barbarians. We found Attila sitting on a wooden chair. We stood at a little distance and Maximin advanced and saluted the barbarian, to whom he gave the Emperor's letter, saying that the Emperor prayed for the safety of him and his."

I will give you now another extract, a description of the banquet which Attila gave:

"The cup-bearers gave us a cup, according to the national custom, that we might pray before we sat down. Having tasted the cup, we proceeded to take our seats; all the chairs were ranged along the walls of the room on either side. Attila sat in the middle on a couch; a second couch was set behind him, and from it steps led up to his bed, which was covered with linen sheets and wrought coverlets for ornament, such as Greeks and Romans use to deck bridal beds. The places on the right of Attila were held chief in honour, those on the left, where we sat, were only second. Berichus, a noble among the Scythians, sat on our side, but had the precedence of us. Onegesius sat on a chair on the right of Attila's couch, and over against Onegesius on a chair sat two of Attila's sons; his eldest son sat on his couch, not near him, but at the extreme end, with his eyes fixed on the ground, in shy respect for his father. When all were arranged, a cup-bearer came and handed Attila a wooden cup of wine. He took it, and saluted the first in precedence, who, honoured by the salutation, stood up, and might not sit down until the king, having tasted or drained the wine, returned the cup to the attendant. All the guests then honoured Attila in the same way, saluting him, and then tasting the cups; but he did not stand up. Each of us had a special cup-bearer, who would come forward in order to present the wine, when the cup-bearer of Attila had retired. When the second in precedence and those next to him had been honoured in like manner, Attila toasted us in the same way according to the order of the seats. When this ceremony was over the cupbearers retired, and tables, large enough for three or four, or even more, to sit at, were placed next the table of Attila, so that each could take of the food on the dishes without leaving his seat. The attendant of Attila first entered with a dish full of meat, and behind him came the other attendants with bread and viands, which they laid on the tables. A luxurious meal, served on silver plate, had been made ready for us and the barbarian guests, but Attila ate nothing but meat on a wooden trencher. In everything else, too, he showed himself temperate; his cup was of wood, while to the guests were given goblets of gold and silver. His dress too, was quite simple, affecting only to be clean. The sword he carried at his side, the latchets of his Scythian shoes, the bridle of his horse were not adorned, like those of the other Scythians, with gold or gems or anything costly. When the viands of the first course had been consumed we all stood up, and did not resume our seats until each one, in the order before observed, drank to the health of Attila in the goblet of wine presented to him. We then sat down, and a second dish was placed on each table with eatables of another kind. After this course the same ceremony was observed as after the first. When evening fell torches were lit, and two barbarians coming forward in front of Attila sang songs they had composed, celebrating his victories and deeds of valour in war. And of the guests, as they looked at the singers, some were pleased with the verses, others reminded of wars were excited in their souls, while yet others, whose bodies were feeble with age and their spirits compelled to rest, shed tears. After the songs a Scythian, whose mind was deranged, appeared, and by uttering outlandish and senseless words forced the company to laugh. After him Zerkon, the Moorish dwarf, entered. He had been sent by Attila as a gift to Aetius, and Edecon had persuaded him to come to Attila in order to recover his wife, whom he had left behind him in Scythia; the lady was a Scythian whom he had obtained in marriage through the influence of his patron Bleda. He did not succeed in recovering her, for Attila was angry with him for returning. On the occasion of the banquet he made his appearance, and threw all except Attila into fits of unquenchable laughter by his appearance, his dress, his voice, and his words, which were a confused jumble of Latin, Hunnic, and Gothic. Attila, however, remained immovable and of unchanging countenance, nor by word or act did he betray anything approaching to a smile of merriment except at the entry of Ernas, his youngest son, whom he pulled by the cheek, and gazed on with a calm look of satisfaction. I was surprised that he made so much of this son, and neglected his other children; but a barbarian who sat beside me and knew Latin, bidding me not reveal what he told, gave me to understand that prophets had forewarned Attila that his race would fall, but would be restored by this boy. When the night had advanced we retired from the banquet, not wishing to assist further at the potations."

Lecture 9:
Attila's Attack on Gaul and Italy

THE INTRIGUES OF HONORIA – THE HUNNIC INVASION OF GAUL – THE INCURSION OF THE HUNS INTO ITALY – DEATH OF ATTILA AND THE COLLAPSE OF THE EMPIRE

THE INTRIGUES OF HONORIA

Since their entry into Europe the Huns had changed in some important ways their life and institutions. They were still a pastoral people; they did not learn to practise tillage; but on the Danube and the Theiss the nomadic habits of the Asiatic steppes were no longer appropriate or necessary. And when they became a political power and had dealings with the Roman Empire – dealings in which diplomacy was required as well as the sword – they found themselves compelled to adapt themselves, however crudely, to the habits of more civilised communities. Attila found that a private secretary who knew Latin was indispensable, and Roman subjects were hired to fill the post. But the most notable fact in the history of the Huns at this period is the ascendancy which their German subjects appear to have gained over them. The most telling sign of this influence is the curious circumstance that some of their kings were called by German names. The names of *Rugila, Mundzuk* (Attila's father), and *Attila* are all German or Germanised. This fact clearly points to intermarriages, but it is also an unconscious acknowledgment by the Huns that their vassals were higher in the scale of civilisation than themselves. If the political situation had remained unchanged for another fifty years the Asiatic invader would probably have been as thoroughly Teutonised as were the Alans, whom the Romans had now come to class among the Germanic peoples.

From A.D. 445 to 450 Attila was at the height of his power: his prestige and influence in Europe were enormous. Up to 448 he exercised his might mainly at the expense of the *eastern* half of the Empire, *i.e.* the provinces and subjects of Theodosius II., from whose government he extorted very large yearly payments of gold. If the western provinces of the Empire until this date escaped the depredations of the Huns, this immunity was mainly due to the personality and policy of Aetius, who always kept on friendly terms with the rulers. But a curious incident happened, when Attila was at the height of his power, which diverted his rapacity from the east to the west, and filled his imagination with a new vision of dominion.

Of the court of Valentinian, of the Emperor's private life, of his relations to his wife and his mother, we know no details. We have seen that he was intellectually and morally feeble, as unfitted for the duties of the throne as had been his uncles Honorius and Arcadius. But his sister Justa Grata Honoria had inherited from her mother some of the qualities we should expect to find in a granddaughter of Theodosius and a great-granddaughter of the first Valentinian. Like Galla Placidia, she was a woman of ambition and self-will. She had been elevated to the rank of an Augusta probably about the same time that the imperial title had been conferred on her brother. During her girlhood, and until Valentinian's marriage, her position in the court was important, but when her nieces were born she had the chagrin of realising that henceforward, from a political and dynastic point of view, she would have to play an obscure part. She would not be allowed to marry anyone except a thoroughly safe man who could be relied upon to entertain no designs upon the throne. We can understand that it must have been highly disagreeable to a woman of her character to see the power in the hands of her brother, immeasurably inferior to herself in brain and energy. She probably felt herself quite as capable of conducting affairs of state as her mother had proved herself to be.

She had passed the age of thirty when her discontent issued in action. She had a separate establishment of her own, within the precincts of the palace, and a comptroller or steward to manage it. His name was Eugenius, and with him she had an amorous intrigue in A.D. 449. She may have been in love with him, but love was subsidiary to the motive of ambition. She designed him to be her instrument in a plot to overthrow her detested brother. The intrigue was discovered, and her paramour was put to death. She was herself driven from the palace, and betrothed compulsorily to a certain Flavius Bassus Herculanus, a rich senator of excellent character, whose sobriety assured the Emperor that a dangerous wife would be unable to draw him into revolutionary schemes. The idea of this union was hateful to Honoria and she bitterly resented the compulsion. She decided to turn for help to a barbarian power. She despatched by the hands of a trustworthy eunuch, Hyacinthus, her ring and a sum of money to Attila, asking him to come to her assistance and prevent the hateful marriage. Attila was the most powerful monarch in Europe, and she boldly chose him to be her champion.

The proposal of the Augusta Honoria was welcome to Attila, and was to determine his policy for the next three years. The message probably reached him in the spring of A.D. 450. The ring had been sent to show that the message was genuine, but Attila interpreted, or chose to interpret, it as a proposal of marriage. He claimed her as his bride, and demanded that half the territory over which Valentinian ruled should be surrendered as her dowry. At the same time he made preparations to invade the western provinces. He addressed his demand not to Valentinian but to the senior Emperor, Theodosius, and Theodosius immediately wrote to Valentinian advising him to hand over Honoria to the Hun. Valentinian was furious. Hyacinthus was tortured to reveal all the details of his mistress's treason, and then beheaded. Galla Placidia had much to do to prevail upon her son to spare his sister's life. When Attila heard how she had been treated, he sent an embassy to Ravenna to protest; the lady, he said, had done no wrong, she was affianced to him, and he would come to enforce her right to a share in the Empire. Attila longed to extend his sway to the shores of the Atlantic, and he would now be able to pretend that Gaul was the portion of Honoria.

THE HUNNIC INVASION OF GAUL

Meanwhile Theodosius had died and his successor, the warlike Marcian, refused in the autumn of A.D. 450 to continue to pay the annual tribute to the Huns. This determined attitude may have helped to decide Attila to turn his arms against the weak realm of Valentinian instead of renewing his attacks upon the exhausted Illyrian lands which he had so often wasted. There was another consideration which urged him to a Gallic campaign. The king of the Vandals had sent many gifts to the king of the Huns and used all his craft to stir him up against the Visigoths. Gaiseric feared the vengeance of Theodoric for the shameful treatment of his daughter, and longed to destroy or weaken the Visigothic nation. We are told by a contemporary writer, who was well informed concerning the diplomatic intrigues at the Hun court, that Attila invaded Gaul "to oblige Gaiseric". But that was only one of his motives. Attila was too wary to unveil his intentions. It was his object to guard against the possibility of the cooperation of the Goths and Romans, and he pretended to be friendly to both. He wrote to Toulouse that his expedition was aimed against the enemies of the Goths, and to Ravenna that he proposed to smite the foes of Rome.

Early in A.D. 451 he set forth with a large army, composed not only of his own Huns, but of the forces of all his German subjects. Prominent among these were the Gepids, from the mountains of Dacia, under their king Ardaric; the Ostrogoths under their three chieftains, Walamir, Thiudemir, and Widimir; the Rugians from the regions of the upper Theiss; the Scirians from Galicia; the Heruls from the shores of the Euxine; the Thuringians, Alans, and others. When they reached the Rhine they were joined by the division of the Burgundians who dwelled to the east of that river and by a portion of the Ripuarian Franks. The army poured into the Belgic provinces, took Metz (April 7), captured many other cities, and laid waste the land. It is not clear whether Aetius had really been lulled into security by the letter of Attila disclaiming any intention of attacking Roman territory. Certainly his preparations seem to have been hurried and made only at the last moment. The troops which he was able to muster were inadequate to meet the huge army of the invader. The federate Salian Franks, some of the Ripuarians, the federate Burgundians of Savoy, and the Celts of Armorica obeyed his summons. But the chance of safety and victory depended on securing the cooperation of the Visigoths, who had decided to remain neutral.

Avitus was chosen by Aetius to undertake the mission of persuading Theodoric. He was successful; but it has been questioned whether his success was due so much to his diplomatic arts as to the fact that Attila was already turning his face towards the Loire. There was a settlement of Alans in the neighbourhood of Valence, and their king had secretly agreed to help Attila to the possession of that city. The objective then of Attila was Orleans, and the first strategic aim of the hastily cemented arrangement between the Romans and Goths was to prevent him from reaching it. The accounts of what happened are contradictory. The truth seems to be that the forces of the allies – the mixed army of Aetius, and the Visigothic host under Theodoric, who was accompanied by his son Thorismund – reached the city before the Huns arrived, and Attila saw that he would only court disaster if he attempted to assault their strongly fortified camp. No course was open but retreat. Aetius had won a bloodless strategic victory (summer, A.D. 451).

It is generally supposed that Attila laid siege to Orleans; but there are two versions. According to one, he was on the point of capturing it when the Roman and Gothic armies appeared, and saved it at the last moment. According to the other, the Huns were already in the town when the rescuers arrived and drove them out. Our sources for both these accounts are certainly derived from ecclesiastical tradition at Orleans; in both of them, the interest is concentrated not on the historical circumstances, but on the wonderful things which were done by the bishop of Orleans, St. Anianus. The tradition used to carry some weight as of early origin, but it was shown some years ago by Krusch to have been a compilation of the eighth century. Our two accounts are simply variants of the same ecclesiastical tradition, which glorified the deeds of St.

Anianus. Are we to choose between these two variants? To my mind, it is entirely uncritical to make such a choice, seeing that the whole tradition is suspicious on account of the obvious motive which it flaunts. There is a third alternative: both accounts may be false. Now when we turn to Jordanes (who wrote a century later), we find not a single word about a siege of Orleans. Orleans comes into the story, but the story, as he tells it, not only omits but clearly excludes a siege. In Jordanes we find Aetius doing exactly what we should have expected; we find him fortifying and strengthening Orleans, before Attila's approach, before there is any collision between the two armies. The relation of Jordanes, as I read it, implies that the army of Aetius and his allies rested on Orleans to oppose the advance of the Huns; and that Attila was not only unable to attack Orleans, but did not venture to advance against a combination more powerful than he had anticipated. He retreated eastward by Tricasses (Troyes). This, I have little doubt, is the true outline of what happened. Orleans was threatened but never besieged – never attacked. But the citizens must have been for some time agitated with the excitement of dread at the approach of a great danger, and in those days of apprehension we may well believe that the bishop of Orleans, Anianus, exercised a beneficial influence in calming the minds of his fellow-citizens and sustaining their bewildered spirits with the hope of divine protection. If the conspicuous activity of the bishop at this crisis produced a deep and abiding effect on the men of Orleans, it is quite in accordance with the growth of legend, of ecclesiastical legend, that the tradition of his good work should have been enhanced, should have been made striking, sensational, and miraculous, by representing the city in the supreme agony of danger – about to be captured or even already captured – and saved by the prayers of the saint. In supporting this view, I may point out that the invasion of Gaul by the Huns stimulated not only the mythopoeic imagination of the Germans, but the mythopoeic inventiveness of the Church. There were probably few cities that came within the actual or possible range of Attila's arm that had not some tale to tell of miraculous intervention. At Paris, which Attila did not approach at all, it was said that St. Geneviève assured the citizens that there was no danger.

It was not enough for the allies to have checked and turned back the invader: they must strike him if possible in his retreat. They overtook him at Troyes, an important meeting-place of roads, and a battle was fought north of the city at the *locus Mauriacus* – which cannot be identified with certainty, but may perhaps be near Mery. The battle, which began in the afternoon and lasted into the night, was drawn; there was immense slaughter, and king Theodoric was among the slain. Next day, the Romans found that Attila was strongly entrenched behind his wagons, and it was said that he had prepared a funeral pyre in which he might perish rather than fall into the hands of his foes. Thorismund, burning to avenge his father's death, was eager to storm the entrenchment. But this did not recommend itself to the policy of Aetius. It was not part of his design to destroy the Hunnic power, of which throughout his career he had made constant use in the interests of the Empire; nor did he desire to increase the prestige of his Visigothic allies. He persuaded Thorismund to return with all haste to Toulouse, lest his brothers should avail themselves of his absence to contest his succession to the kingship. He also persuaded the Franks to return immediately to their own land. Disembarrassed of these auxiliaries, he was able to pursue his own policy and permit Attila to escape with the remnant of his host.

This battle has been generally misnamed the battle of Chalons, but Chalons (Catalauni) is far away; it would be much more correct to call it the battle of Troyes. Both sides sustained great losses, but in the given circumstances it was a triumph for the defenders of Gaul, and it hastened the retreat of the invader. But I would have you observe that strategically it only reinforced the check which the Huns had already received, and merely accelerated their departure. It inflicted an actual blow by the losses which at the lowest estimate must have been heavy; but its chief importance was undoubtedly the moral injury which it dealt to the prestige of Attila's power. If Aetius had permitted him to retreat, unassailed and at his leisure, the moral effect of the check would have been infinitely smaller; and this was probably the main consideration which influenced Aetius in courting a battle. It is essential to realise that the battle of the *locus*

Mauriacus was not a battle of despair; and I think that we may be certain that the odds were not against Aetius, or he would not have risked it.

Under this criticism, the battle cannot retain precisely the historical significance which has commonly been claimed for it. It is usually ranked among the great battles which have decided the fates of nations and determined the course of history. But the fate of Attila's invasion was decided before the battle was fought; it was decided by the strategic dispositions of Aetius. Nothing but an annihilating victory for Attila would have changed the situation, and on general grounds it is improbable that Aetius plunged into very serious risks or hazards. His strategy had already been decisively superior, and all our evidence seems to me to point to the fact that Attila had no great strategical talent. Contrast the futility of this Mongolian invasion of Gaul with the splendidly conceived and splendidly executed strategy which marked the great invasion of eastern Europe in the middle of the thirteenth century. Such a contrast illustrates the truth of what I say, that Attila was no strategist – a fact which has not been hitherto duly estimated.

But if we deny to the battle of Troyes its claim to be one of the great decisive battles of history, you will expect me to transfer to the whole campaign the significance which I have ventured to deny to the isolated engagement. But can the invasion and the campaign regarded as a whole be said to assume the proportions of an ecumenical crisis? The danger did not mean so much as has been commonly assumed. If Attila had been victorious; if he had defeated the Romans and the Goths at Orleans; if he had held Gaul at his mercy and had translated – and we have no evidence that this was his design – the seat of his government and the abode of his people from the Theiss to the Seine or the Loire, there is no reason to suppose that the course of history would have been seriously altered. For the rule of the Huns in Gaul could only have been a matter of a year or two; it could not have survived the death of the great king on whose brains and personal character it depended. Without depreciating the achievement of Aetius and Theodoric, we must recognise that at worst the danger they averted was of a totally different order from the issues which were at stake on the fields of Plataea and the Metaurus. If Attila had succeeded in his campaign, he would probably have been able to compel the surrender of Honoria, and if a son had been born of their marriage and proclaimed Augustus in Gaul, the Hun might have been able to exercise considerable influence on the fortunes of that country; but that influence would probably not have been anti-Roman.

THE INCURSION OF THE HUNS INTO ITALY

Attila lost little time in seeking to take revenge for the unexpected blow which had been dealt him. He again came forward as the champion of the Augusta Honoria, claiming her as his affianced bride, and invaded Italy in the following year (A.D. 452). Aquileia, the city of the Venetian march, now fell before the Huns, and was razed to the ground, never to rise again: in the next century hardly a trace of it could be seen. Verona and Vicentia did not share this fate, but they were exposed to the violence of the invader, while Ticinum and Mediolanum were compelled to purchase exemption from fire and sword.

The path of Attila was now open to Rome. Aetius, with whatever forces he could muster, might hang upon his line of march, but was not strong enough to risk a battle. But the lands south of the Po, and Rome herself, were spared the presence of the Huns. According to tradition, the thanks of Italy were on this occasion due not to Aetius, but to Leo, the bishop of Rome. The Emperor, who was at Rome, sent Leo and two leading senators, Avienus and Trygetius, to negotiate with the invader. Trygetius had diplomatic experience; he had negotiated the treaty with Gaiseric in A.D. 435. Leo was an imposing figure, and the story gives him the credit for having persuaded Attila to retreat. He was supported by celestial beings; the apostles Peter and Paul are said to have appeared to Attila and by their threats terrified him into leaving the soil of Italy.

The fact of the embassy cannot be doubted. The distinguished ambassadors visited the Huns' camp near the south shore of Lake Garda. It is also certain that Attila suddenly retreated. But we are at a loss to know what considerations were offered him to induce him to depart. It is unreasonable to suppose that this heathen king would have cared for the thunders or persuasions of the Church. The Emperor refused to surrender Honoria, and it is not recorded that money was paid. A trustworthy chronicle hands down another account which does not conflict with the fact that an embassy was sent, but evidently furnishes the true reasons which moved Attila to receive it favourably. Plague broke out in the barbarian host and their food ran short, and at the same time troops arrived from the east, sent by Marcian to the aid of Italy. If his host was suffering from pestilence, and if troops arrived from the east, we can understand that Attila was forced to withdraw. But, whatever terms were arranged, he did not pretend that they meant a permanent peace. The question of Honoria was left unsettled, and he threatened that he would come again and do worse things in Italy unless she were given up with the due portion of the imperial possessions.

DEATH OF ATTILA AND THE COLLAPSE OF THE EMPIRE

Attila survived his Italian expedition only one year. His attendants found him dead one morning, and the bride whom he had married the day before sitting beside his bed in tears. His death was ascribed to the bursting of an artery, but it was also rumoured that he had been slain by the woman in his sleep.

With the death of Attila, the Empire of the Huns, which had no natural cohesion, was soon scattered to the winds. Among the dead king's numerous children there was none of commanding ability, none who had the strength to remove his brothers and step into his father's place. Hence the sons proposed to divide the inheritance into portions. This was the opportunity of their German vassals, who did not choose to allow themselves to be allotted to various masters like herds of cattle. The rebellion was led by Ardaric, the Gepid, Attila's chief adviser. In Pannonia near the river Nedao another battle of the nations was fought, and the coalition of German vassals – Gepids, Ostrogoths, Rugians, Heruls, and the rest – utterly defeated the host of their Hun lords (A.D. 454). It is not improbable that the Germans received encouragement and support from the Emperor Marcian.

This cardinal event led to considerable changes in the geographical distribution of the barbarian peoples. The Huns themselves were scattered far and wide. Some remained in the west, but the greater part of them fled to the regions north of the lower Danube, where we shall presently find them, under two of Attila's sons, playing a part in the troubled history of the Thracian provinces. The Gepids extended their power over the whole of Dacia (Siebenburgen), along with the plains between the Theiss and the Danube which had been the habitation of the Huns. The Emperor Marcian was deeply interested in the new disposition of the German nations, and his diplomacy aimed at arranging them in such a way that they would mutually check each other. He seems to have made an alliance with the Gepids which proved exceptionally permanent. He assigned to the Ostrogoths settlements in northern Pannonia, as federates of the Empire. The Rugians found new abodes on the north banks of the Danube, opposite to Noricum, where they also were for some years federates of Rome. The Scirians settled farther east, and were the northern neighbours and foes of the Ostrogoths in Pannonia; and the Heruls found territory in the same vicinity – perhaps between the Scirians and Rugians. But from all these peoples there was a continual flow into the Roman Empire of men seeking military service. In the depopulated provinces of Illyricum and Thrace there was room and demand for new settlers. Rugians were settled in Bizye and Arcadiopolis; Scirians in Lower Moesia.

The battle of the Nedao was an arbitrament far more momentous than the battle of Troyes. The catastrophe of the Hun power was indeed inevitable, for the social fabric of the Huns and all their social instincts were opposed to the concentration and organisation which could alone maintain the permanence of their empire. But it was not the less important that the catastrophe arrived at this particular moment – important both for the German peoples and for the Empire. Although the Hunnic power disappeared, at one stroke, into the void from which it had so suddenly arisen, we shall see, if we reflect for a moment, that it affected profoundly the course of history. The invasion of the nomads in the fourth century had precipitated the Visigoths from Dacia into the Balkan peninsula, had led to the disaster of Hadrianople, and may be said to have determined the whole chain of Visigothic history. But, apart from this special consequence of the Hun invasion, the Hun empire performed a function of much greater significance in European history. It helped to retard the whole process of the German dismemberment of the Empire. It did this in two ways: in the first place, by controlling many of the East German peoples beyond the Danube, from whom the Empire had most to fear; and in the second place by constantly supplying Roman generals with auxiliaries who proved an invaluable resource in the struggle with the German enemies. The devastations which some of the Roman provinces suffered from the Huns in the last years of Theodosius II. and Valentinian III. must be esteemed a loss which was more than set off by the support which Hunnic arms had for many years lent to the Empire, especially if we consider that, as subsequent events showed, the Germans would have committed the same depredations if the Huns had not been there. This retardation of the process of dismemberment, enabling the imperial government to maintain itself for a longer period in those lands which were destined ultimately to become Teutonic kingdoms, was all in the interest of civilisation; for the Germans, who in almost all cases were forced to establish their footing on imperial territory as *federates* , and who then by degrees converted this dependent relation into independent sovranty, were more likely to gain some faint apprehension of Roman order, some slight taste for Roman civilisation, than if their careers of conquest had been less gradual and impeded.

Lecture 10:
Decline of the Roman Power in the West

INFLUENCE OF THE VANDAL OCCUPATION OF AFRICA – RICIMER AND THE LAST PHANTOM EMPERORS IN THE WEST – GUNDOBAD AND ORESTES IN ITALY – DEPOSITION OF ROMULUS AUGUSTULUS AND ITS SIGNIFICANCE – ODOVACAR, PATRICIAN AND KING IN ITALY

INFLUENCE OF THE VANDAL OCCUPATION OF AFRICA

The collapse of the Huns at the battle of Nedao (A.D. 454) was immediately followed by the settlement of the Ostrogoths in Pannonia, from which they were soon to repeat, in some sort, the part of their old brethren the Visigoths and assist in the disintegration of Roman dominion. The Gepids established their kingdom in Dacia, and we may mark this as the fifth stage in the history of that country, which had been successively submitted to the Dacians, the Romans, the Visigoths, the Huns, and now the Gepids. The Rugians, another East German people, settled along the Danube, probably between Linz and Vienna.

The forty years succeeding the collapse of the Empire of the Huns, from about 454 to 493, were marked by the gradual advance of the German power in Gaul and Spain; while before 493 Italy itself had become a German kingdom. Now the steady increase of the barbarian power, and the steady decline of the imperial power, in the west during these years was largely conditioned (as was noted in an earlier lecture) by the existence and hostility of the Vandal power in north Africa. The Vandal king Gaiseric had formed a strong fleet with which he was able to attack and plunder Italy, as well as to occupy Sicily and Sardinia. I may here make a remark on the general significance of the Vandals in European history. Their kingdom lasted for just a hundred years. Then it was reconquered by the Empire, and the Vandal name disappeared from among the nations. What, then, was the historical significance of this people? Apart from devastation and destruction, what did they contribute, did they contribute anything, towards the permanent shaping of Europe? The destinies of Spain were not seriously affected by their settlement, which in the case of that country amounted to little more than a transit. The fortunes of Spain could not have been very different if the Vandals had never set foot in the peninsula. Nevertheless I conceive that the Vandals were an important factor, though they built up no abiding kingdom. Their occupation of Africa; the strong and formidable, though only temporary power which Gaiseric established at Carthage, supported by the sea-power which he organised in the Mediterranean – these were circumstances of inestimable consequence for the development of events in Europe. The presence of this enemy in Africa – and Gaiseric proved an enemy more irreconcilable than any other German foe – immeasurably weakened the Roman power in all the western provinces. It had the direct result of controlling the corn supply of Italy, and it prevented the Roman government from acting with effectual vigour in either Gaul or Spam. If the Romans had continued to hold Africa – if the Vandals had not been there – there can be little doubt that the imperial power would have maintained itself for a far longer period in Italy, and would have offered far more effective opposition to the expansion of the Germans in Gaul and Spain. In my view, therefore, the contribution which the Vandals made to the shaping of Europe was this: the very existence of their kingdom in Africa, and of their naval power in the Mediterranean, acted as a powerful protection for the growth of the new German kingdoms in Gaul and Spain, and ultimately helped the founding of a German kingdom in Italy, by dividing, diverting, and weakening the forces of the Empire. The Vandals had got round, as it were, to the rear of the Empire; and the effect of their powerful presence there was enhanced by the hostile and aggressive attitude which they continuously adopted.

RICIMER AND THE LAST PHANTOM EMPERORS IN THE WEST

Even if there had been united councils in Italy, the task of ubiquitous defence would have been beyond the power of the government; but the government went to pieces, and thereby hastened the dismemberment. I need not here enter at all into the history of the short-reigned emperors who were set up and knocked down in Italy after the murder of Valentinian III. in 455. I would invite your attention to two main points: first, the Vandal danger which embarrassed the Italian government during these years; and, secondly, the power behind the imperial throne. This power behind the throne is of great significance for our present purpose. It was wielded by a German general, Ricimer, of Suevian race. He was the successor of the German Stilicho and of the Roman Aetius as the defender of the Empire. The circumstances in which Ricimer had to act were indeed different from the circumstances of Stilicho and of Aetius. They differed in two main particulars. First, as I have already mentioned, while the activity of Stilicho and of Aetius reached beyond Italy to the other western provinces, the activity of Ricimer was practically confined to Italy and the Italian seas: this was due to the powerful hostility of the Vandals. Secondly, Stilicho and Aetius had been the ministers of emperors who belonged to the well-established dynasty of Theodosius; and although those emperors, Honorius and Valentinian III., were personally weak and worthless, yet their legitimacy gave their thrones stability; so that Stilicho and Aetius could feel that, though they might fall themselves, they had a secure throne behind them. It was not so in the case of Ricimer. The male line of Theodosius was extinct; Valentinian III. had left no sons: and it devolved upon Ricimer to provide the imperial authority which he was to serve. He became through circumstances an emperor-maker; and his difficulty was this. If he set up too strong a man, his own power would have probably been overridden; his own fall would have been the consequence; while on the other hand weak upstarts were unable to maintain their position for any length of time, since public opinion did not respect them. In estimating the part played by Ricimer, I think that hard and unjust measure is sometimes dealt out to him. The difficulties of his position can hardly be over-stated, and he may be held to have made a serious and honest attempt to perform the task of preserving a government in Italy and defending the peninsula against its formidable enemies.

Now you must observe that the fact of Ricimer's being a German was a significant and determining factor in the situation. If he had not been a German, the situation would have been much simpler; for he could have assumed the imperial purple himself; the real and the nominal power would have been combined in the same hands; and the problem of government would have been solved. His German birth excluded this solution. This is a very remarkable thing. Germans like Stilicho and Ricimer, who attained to the highest posts in the imperial service, who might even intermarry with the imperial house, could not venture to take the last great step and mount the imperial throne. Just so much, just at the pinnacle, they were still outsiders. And they fully recognised this disability themselves. An Emperor Ricimer would have seemed to all men, and to Ricimer himself, impossible. This disability still resting upon men of pure German descent within the Empire, and their own deference to the prevailing sentiment, are highly significant.

It is also to be noted that in the intervals between the reigns of the emperors whom Ricimer set up and pulled down, when there was no emperor regnant in Italy, it did not mean that there was no emperor at all. At such times the imperial authority was entirely invested in the eastern emperor who reigned at Constantinople, the Emperor Leo; and this, too, was fully acknowledged by Ricimer, who indeed selected two of his emperors by arrangement with Leo.

GUNDOBAD AND ORESTES IN ITALY

Ricimer died in 472 and the march of affairs after his death shows how difficult his task had been. The events of these next few years have often been misconceived in respect of the exact nature of their importance. Ricimer's nephew Gundobad seemed marked out to succeed to the place of his uncle – as the head of the military forces in Italy, and as the power behind the throne. Gundobad belonged to the royal family of the Burgundians and was a son of the reigning Burgundian king; but he had entered the imperial service. The Emperor Olybrius, Ricimer's last creation, recognised Gundobad's position and raised him to the rank of patrician. But Olybrius died before the end of the year, and a crisis ensued. For Gundobad and the Emperor Leo could not agree as to who should succeed to the purple. Leo's candidate was Julius Nepos, and Gundobad set up an obscure person named Glycerius. This situation illustrates, I think, a great merit of Ricimer, viz. his diplomatic success in dealing with the court of Constantinople, and in keeping on good terms with Leo. The importance of this part of his policy is conditioned by the common danger from the Vandals, which the eastern provinces had to fear as well as the western, though to a smaller extent.

But hardly had the deadlock arisen between Gundobad and the Emperor Leo, when Gundobad disappeared from the scene. A new ambition was suddenly opened to him, more alluring than the government of Italy, viz. the government of his father's Burgundian realm – a realm which was still nominally an imperial dependency. His father had died, and Gundobad withdrew to Burgundy to endeavour to secure his own election. He succeeded, and we shall meet him hereafter on the Burgundian throne. After his departure the Emperor Julius Nepos, Leo's candidate, landed in Italy and deposed Glycerius. But Nepos was not equal to the situation. He very wisely negotiated a peace with Euric, king of the West Goths, of whose reign I shall presently have to speak; and he then appointed a certain Roman, Orestes by name, to be commander-in-chief, *magister militum* , in Gaul, to defend the Roman territory there. Orestes had been in Attila's service: he had lived much with barbarians of all kinds, and Nepos thought that he was making a very clever choice in selecting Orestes to command an army of barbarian soldiers. I may point out that after the break-up of Attila's empire there had been an immense influx of barbarian mercenaries into the Roman service. The army which Orestes now commanded was composed not only of Germans drawn from families long settled in the Empire but also of these new adventurers who had drifted into Italy through Noricum and Pannonia. Nepos was deceived in Orestes; Orestes was ambitious, and instead of going to Gaul, as he had been told, he marched on Ravenna. Nepos immediately fled to Dalmatia. Italy was for the moment in the power of Orestes. He did not seize the Empire himself, he preferred the double arrangement which had prevailed in the time of Ricimer, though there was not now the same necessity for it. Keeping the military power himself, he invested his child-son Romulus Augustulus with the imperial purple. But before Orestes had established his government he was surprised by a new situation. His host of barbarian soldiers, who were largely Heruls, suddenly formulated a demand. They were dissatisfied with the arrangements for quartering them. Their wives and children lived in the garrison towns in their neighbourhood, but they had no proper homes or hearths. The idea occurred to them that arrangements might be made in their behalf in Italy similar to those which had been made in Gaul, for instance, in behalf of the Visigoths and the Burgundians. Why should not they obtain permanent quarters, abiding homes, on the large estates, the *latifundia* , of Italy? This feeling prevailed in the host, and the officers formulated a demand which they laid before Orestes. The demand simply was that the normal system of *hospitalitas* should be adopted in Italy for their benefit, *i.e.* that a third part of the Italian soil should be divided among them. The sympathies or prejudices of Orestes were too Roman to let him entertain this demand; Italy had so far been sacrosanct from barbarian settlements. He refused, and his refusal led to a revolution. The mercenary soldiers found a leader in an officer who was thoroughly representative of themselves, an adventurer who had come from beyond the Danube to seek his fortunes, and had entered the service of the Empire. This was Odovacar: he was probably a Scirian, possibly a Rugian (there is a discrepancy in the authorities), at all events he belonged to one of the smaller East German peoples who had originally come from regions on the lower Oder, had formed part of Attila's empire, and had partly settled on the middle Danube, partly entered Roman service after the fall of that empire. Odovacar now undertook to realise the claim of the soldiers, and consequently there was a revolution. Orestes was put to death, and his son the Emperor Romulus Augustulus abdicated. The power in Italy was in the hands of Odovacar. We are in the year 476.

DEPOSITION OF ROMULUS AUGUSTULUS AND ITS SIGNIFICANCE

Now what I would have you specially observe is that there was, constitutionally speaking, nothing novel in the situation. There were two legitimate emperors, the Emperor Zeno at Constantinople, and the Emperor Julius Nepos (who was in Dalmatia). In the eyes of the government of Constantinople, Romulus Augustulus was a usurper. This usurper had now been deposed by a military revolution; the leader of that revolution, Odovacar, had shown no disloyalty to the eastern emperor, whose authority he fully acknowledged. There was no thought here of any dismemberment, or detachment, or breaking away from the Empire. Odovacar was a Roman officer, he was raised by the army into the virtual position of a *magister militum* , and his first thought, after the revolution had been carried through, was to get his position regularised by imperial authority, to gain from Zeno a formal recognition and appointment. Odovacar was in fact the successor of the series of German commanders who had supported the Empire for eighty years: and when he came to power in 476, there was not the least reason in the actual circumstances why the same kind of regime should not have been continued as in the days of Ricimer. But Odovacar had statesmanlike qualities, and he decided against the system of Ricimer, which had proved thoroughly unsatisfactory and unstable. His idea was to rule Italy under the imperial authority of Constantinople, unhampered by a second emperor in Italy, whom recent experiences had shown to be worse than useless. There would have been no difficulty for Odovacar in adopting this policy, if there had existed no second emperor at the time; but Julius Nepos was still alive, and, what was most important, he had been recognised at Constantinople. Odovacar was determined *not* to acknowledge the authority of Nepos. It is very important to understand this element in the situation, because it directly led to the peculiar position which Odovacar afterwards occupied. He first addressed himself to the Roman senate, and caused that body to send envoys to Constantinople, bearing the imperial insignia, and a letter to the Emperor Zeno. The purport of the letter was to suggest that one emperor, namely Zeno himself and his successors at Constantinople, sufficed for the needs of the whole Empire, and to ask that Zeno should authorise Odovacar to conduct the administration in Italy, and should confer on him the title of Patricius, which had been borne by Ricimer. The Emperor was not a little embarrassed. Julius Nepos was at the same time demanding his help to recover Italy, and Nepos had a legitimate claim. The Emperor wrote a very diplomatic reply. He insisted, in the most definite and correct terms, on the legal claim of Nepos; he, however, told Odovacar, whom he praised for the consideration he had shown in his dealings with the Italians after the revolution, that he would confer upon him the title of Patricius, if Nepos had not already done so.

This limited recognition was not what Odovacar had hoped for; the express reserve of the rights of Julius Nepos was most unsatisfactory; there was always a chance that those rights might at a favourable moment be enforced. Accordingly, while he accepted the patriciate from Zeno, and so legitimised his position as an imperial minister in the eyes of Italy, he fortified himself by assuming another title which must have expressed his relation to the barbarian army, viz. the title of king, *rex* . We do not know what solemnity or form accompanied the assumption of this title. But its effect was to give Odovacar the double character of a German king as well as an imperial officer. A close parallel to this double position is that of Alaric at the close of the fourth century. He was king of the Goths, but at the same time he was *magister militum* in Illyricum. So Odovacar was king of the Germans who through him obtained settlements in Italy, while he was also a Patricius, acting under the authority of the Emperor Zeno. There was thus theoretically no detachment of Italy from the Empire in the days of Odovacar any more than there had been a detachment of Illyricum in the days of Alaric. The position of Odovacar was still further regularised a few years later (480) by the death of Julius Nepos.

The death of Julius Nepos is an event which has some significance; it marks the cessation of a separate line of emperors in the west. But if I have made clear the circumstances of the revolution headed by Odovacar, you will perceive that this event, though of importance in the history of Italy, has not the importance and significance which has been commonly ascribed to it. The year 476 has been generally taken as a great landmark, and the event has been commonly described as the fall of the Western Empire. This unfortunate expression conveys a wholly erroneous idea of the bearings of Odovacar's revolution. Let me observe in the first place that the expression 'Western Empire' is constitutionally improper; it may be convenient as a loose expression for the western provinces of the Empire which, since Theodosius the Great, had been ruled by an emperor at Rome or Ravenna; but there was only one empire, and at the time no one would have dreamed of talking of two. On several occasions during the fifth century the death or deposition of an emperor at Rome or Ravenna had been followed by a considerable space of time in which no successor was elected. During such time the supremacy and authority of the emperor at Constantinople were always acknowledged. Now at any of those times it would have been quite possible for the emperor at Constantinople to have asserted his authority in the western provinces, or for Italy and the western provinces to have said to him: "We do not want a second emperor; you are sufficient." And if such a thing had happened, no one could have possibly described it as a fall of the Western Empire. Yet what happened in 476 was exactly analogous. In the second place, this event concerns specially the history of Italy, in the same way as the settlements of the Visigoths and Burgundians concerned the history of Gaul; and the settlement of the Germans in Italy does not directly affect the western provinces as a whole. It is then a misleading misuse of words to speak of a fall of the Western Empire in 476: the revolution of that year marks but a stage, and that not the last stage, in the encroachments of the barbarian settlers in the western provinces.

Odovacar was not hampered, as Ricimer had been, by the nominal authority of a resident emperor; he was able to pursue his own policy without any embarrassment, and to act as an independent ruler. His policy was one of peace; he was entirely averse from aggression. It must be noted, too, that his position was much easier than that of Ricimer, because the Vandal hostilities had ceased. Gaiseric had died in 477; and two years before his death he had made peace with Rome, and Odovacar had induced him to restore Sicily in return for a yearly payment. The cessation of the Vandal danger was of immense importance for Odovacar's government; the only task before it which involved warfare was to meet a danger which threatened on the northern frontier of Italy. This danger sprang from the kingdom of the Rugians on the Danube, to the north of Noricum. The Danubian provinces were completely disorganised; government had practically ceased; and the provincials were exposed not only to the oppression of the Rugians but to the incursions of other Germans – Alamanni, Thuringians, and Heruls. There is a famous work which gives a very vivid picture of the condition of Noricum and the adjacent lands at this period. It is the *Life of St. Severinus*, written a few years later by Eugippius, and I recommend it to your attention. Severinus was the only protection the provincials had, except the walls of their towns; he was a powerful protector, for he exercised immense influence upon the barbarians. This influence, due to his strong personality and his devoted life, was increased by a belief in his miraculous powers and prophetic faculty. But though the self-sacrificing efforts of this monk did something to alleviate the condition of those lands and to restrain the cruelties of the barbarians, the miseries of the time in that quarter of Europe can hardly be exaggerated. Odovacar came to the rescue. He overthrew the Rugian kingdom, which had no elements of strength, and he removed the Roman provincials from the dangerous frontier to the shelter of Italy.

ODOVACAR, PATRICIAN AND KING IN ITALY

I must return to the settlement of the barbarians in Italy which was carried out by Odovacar. Two-thirds of their estates were left to the Italian proprietors; one-third was taken from them and assigned to the German soldiers, who were thus distributed throughout Italy. These soldiers were mainly East Germans; there was thus an East German colonisation of Italy. It differed from the settlements of the Visigoths and Burgundians in Gaul, in so far as the German settlers were limited to no special provinces, but were scattered throughout the peninsula among the inhabitants. Now I should like to emphasise here again the important fact to which I have before called attention, that these divisions of land among the barbarians were simply an extension of the old Roman system of quartering soldiers. For the continuity comes out with special force in the case of Odovacar's land-division in Italy. In the time of Stilicho, and throughout the fifth century, urban householders were obliged by law to vacate a third part of their houses to the soldiers who were stationed in the towns. This law was passed by Arcadius and Honorius; it was reinforced by Theodosius II. and Valentinian III.; it was afterwards received into the Code of Justinian. The troops therefore who were commanded by Orestes must have been quartered in the Italian towns on this principle. When therefore they demanded a third part of the land they were simply demanding an extension of the quartering system, the *hospitalitas* – an extension such as had already been carried out in other provinces. This case therefore illustrates with particular clearness the great and important principle that these concessions of land are all based on the military quartering system of Rome.

It is obvious that the order of things introduced by Odovacar could hardly be permanent. His position was essentially weak. He was a patrician and he was a king, but in neither capacity had he any firm support. He had received from Constantinople only a reserved recognition; and as a German king he had no people. For the Germans to whom he owed his elevation were a mixed company of adventurers, fragments of many folks; there was no close or intimate bond among them, no national feeling. Odovacar, however, attempted and not unsuccessfully to found his power on closer co-operation with the senate.

The regime was in its very nature transitory. Its significance is twofold; on the one hand as a continuation of the regime of Ricimer – this side is represented by Odovacar in his character of patrician; on the other hand, as preparing for the foundation of a true German kingdom in Italy – this side is represented in his character as king.

Lecture 11:
The Ostrogothic Conquest of Italy

THE EARLY LIFE OF THEODERIC THE OSTROGOTH – THE OVERTHROW OF ODOVACAR IN ITALY – THE COMPLETION OF THE OSTROGOTHIC CONQUEST – THE OSTROGOTHIC CONSTITUTION – THE REIGN OF THEODERIC

THE EARLY LIFE OF THEODERIC THE OSTROGOTH

After the overthrow of the Hunnic Empire on the field of Nadao in A.D. 454 the Ostrogoths, who had been one of the chief members of that Empire, settled in Pannonia. Now for the first time they settled on the inner side of the Roman frontier. The settlement was made by agreement with the Emperor Marcian, and the Ostrogoths then became *federates* of the Empire. The Ostrogoths were *not* at this time under the rule of a single or predominant national king. No leader held among them the place which Hermanric had held in the fourth century. Monarchy had not developed in their case as it had developed with the Visigoths; and this is quite what we might have expected; for they had been all this time under the domination of the Huns, and it would have been obviously the policy of the Hunnic kings to encourage division rather than unity. Accordingly we find the Ostrogoths under a number of kings, prominent among whom were three brothers of the royal race of the Amals. The name of one of these brothers was Thiudemir; and the story runs that on the very day on which the news of the great victory of Nadao came to the house of Thiudemir, a son was born to him. This son was *Thiuda-reiks* ('ruler of the people'), a name which was corrupted in Greek and Roman mouths into Theuderic or Theoderic. The story reminds us of the similar anecdote that Alexander the Great was born on the day on which his father's general won a victory over the Illyrians. Whenever Alexander's birthday was – the exact date is unknown – it was certainly within a few months of that victory; and we shall not be wrong in assuming that Theoderic was born in the chronological neighbourhood of the battle of Nadao, somewhere about the year 454. He was sent in his boyhood as a hostage to Constantinople, where he learned to know and appreciate Roman civilisation and Roman institutions, although he did not abandon the Arian faith in which he had been brought up. He returned home in 470 or 471, at the age of sixteen or seventeen, and in 471 he was elected a king. We can be certain about this date, because thirty years later, in the year 500, when he was lord of Italy, he celebrated his *tricennalia* , that is the thirtieth anniversary of his election as king. But it is to be observed that neither he nor his father, who was still alive, was king of the Ostrogothic nation; they were simply petty kings, *gaukönige* .

Immediately after this election, Thiudemir and his son Theoderic led their portion of the Ostrogothic people southward into the Balkan peninsula, and forced the Emperor Leo to grant them new settlements in Macedonia – in the original Macedonia near the sea. Their territory included the cities of Pella, Pydna, and Methone. After Thiudemir's death Theoderic reigned alone, and the next years were marked by his rivalry and struggle with another Ostrogothic chief of the same name who had also settled in the Balkan peninsula. It was a triangular struggle between the two rival Gothic chiefs and the Emperor Zeno, and the relations among the three vary and change like the figures of a kaleidoscope. I believe that the object of Theoderic's ambition, like the first object of Alaric's ambition, was to be appointed *magister militum* . In the year 483, after his rival's death, he obtained this coveted post, and was created *magister militum praesentalis* . In the following year, he was honoured by the consulship. He now, like Alaric, stood in a double relation to his people: he was not only their king; they were also bound to obey him as imperial commander-in-chief. But the new *magister militum* was still a thorn in the side of the Empire; he quarrelled with the Emperor in 487, revolted, and marched with his Ostrogoths to the walls of Constantinople. The Emperor now reached the conviction that the presence of the Ostrogoths and the Ostrogothic *magister militum* in the Illyrian provinces could never be placed on a satisfactory basis, and would be a constant source of trouble and danger. Could any expedient be found for getting rid of them? The idea occurred that a profitable and tempting task might be imposed upon the *magister militum* which would finally deliver Constantinople and the Illyrian provinces of his presence. He might be sent to Italy to conquer and displace Odovacar. Our material is too scanty to enable us to say whether Zeno adopted this resolution merely as an expedient to remove Theoderic, or whether he had already independently cherished the notion of interfering in the regime of Italy, and perhaps of resuming the peninsula under his immediate rule. Odovacar was nominally his vice-regent, a *magister militum* of the

Empire; but Zeno had never given him a wholehearted or unreserved recognition. One of our chief authorities tells us that Zeno intended ultimately to go to Italy himself. The words (which some historians have failed to understand) are these: "The Emperor made a bargain with Theoderic: if he (Theoderic) overcame Odovacar, he should (as a reward for his services) rule provisionally in Italy until he (Zeno) should come (*dum adveniret*)." I see no reason for rejecting this statement, but we must be careful how we interpret it. It need not seem that Zeno had made up his mind to go to Italy or resume in his own hands the immediate government. It may have been simply the official and diplomatic way in which the bargain was expressed, so as to reserve the imperial rights, and make it clear that, while Theoderic succeeded to the quasi-imperial power wielded by Odovacar, he was still responsible to the Emperor, who would at any moment have the right to recall him or suspend him.

THE OVERTHROW OF ODOVACAR IN ITALY

Theoderic accepted the mission which was destined to lead him to a great place in history. He started for Italy in 488. It is curious how the fortunes of the Ostrogoths seemed to repeat the fortunes of the Visigoths. Nearly a hundred years after the Visigoths had been temporarily settled as *federates* in the Ilyrian peninsula, the Ostrogoths were for a brief period settled there too. The Visigoths had ravaged and vexed the provinces, until finally King Alaric had been made a *magister militum* ; the Ostrogoths a century later did exactly the same thing, and King Theoderic, like Alaric, was in his turn made a *magister militum* . Then Theoderic, again like Alaric, migrated with his people to Italy.

It was not till the end of August (A.D. 489) that, having crossed the Julian Alps, the Ostrogoths reached the river Sontius (Isonzo), and that the struggle for Italy began. Of this memorable war we have only the most meagre outline. The result was decided within twelve months, but three and a half years were to elapse before the last resistance of Odovacar was broken down and Theoderic was completely master of Italy.

It was perhaps where the Sontius and the Frigidus meet that Theoderic found Odovacar in a carefully fortified camp, prepared to oppose his entry into Venetia. Odovacar had considerable forces, for besides his own army he had succeeded in enlisting foreign help. We are not told who his allies were: we can only guess that among them may have been the Burgundians, who, as we know, helped him at a later stage. The battle was fought on August 28; Odovacar was defeated and compelled to retreat, his next line of defence was on the Athesis (Adige), and he fortified himself in a camp close to Verona, with the river behind him. Here the second battle of the war was fought a month later (about September 20) and resulted in a decisive victory for Theoderic. The carnage of Odovacar's men is said to have been immense; but they fought desperately and the Ostrogothic losses were severe; the river was fed with corpses. The defeated king himself fled to Ravenna. The greater part of his army, with Tufa who held the highest command, surrendered to Theoderic, who immediately proceeded to Milan.

Northern Italy was now at the feet of the Goth; Rome and Sicily were prepared to submit, and it looked as though nothing remained to complete the conquest but the capture of Ravenna. But the treachery of Tufa changed the situation. Theoderic imprudently trusted him, and sent him with his own troops and a few distinguished Ostrogoths against Odovacar. At Faventia (Faenza) Tufa espoused again the cause of his old master and handed over to him the Goths, who were put into irons.

Theoderic made Ticinum (Pavia) his headquarters during the winter, and it is said that one of his motives for choosing this city was to cultivate the friendship of the old bishop Epiphanius, who had great influence with Odovacar. In the following year Odovacar was able to take the field again, to seize Cremona and Milan, and to blockade his adversary in Ticinum. At this juncture the Visigoths came to the help of the Ostrogoths and sent an army into Italy. The siege was raised, and the decisive battle of the war was fought on the river Addua (Adda), a battle in which Odovacar was utterly defeated (August 11, A.D. 490). He fled for the second time to Ravenna. It was probably this victory that decided the Roman senate to abandon the cause of Odovacar, and to accept Theoderic. It made him master of Rome, southern Italy, and Sicily.

The agreement that Zeno made with Theoderic had been secret and unofficial. The Emperor had done nothing directly to break off his relations with Odovacar. But Odovacar seems some time before the battle of the Addua to have courted a formal rupture. He created his son Thela a Caesar, and this was equivalent to renouncing his subordination to the Emperor and declaring Italy independent. He probably calculated that in the strained relations which then existed between the Italian Catholics and the Greek East, on account of an ecclesiastical schism, the policy of cutting the rope which bound Italy to Constantinople would be welcomed at Rome and throughout the provinces. The senators may have been divided on this issue, but the battle of the Addua decided them as a body to 'betray' Odovacar, and before the end of the year Festus, the *princeps* of the senate, went to Constantinople to announce the success of Theoderic, and to arrange the conditions of the new Italian government.

THE COMPLETION OF THE OSTROGOTHIC CONQUEST

Theoderic confidently believed that his task was now virtually finished. But the cause of his thrice-defeated enemy was not yet hopelessly lost. Tufa was still at large with troops at his command; and various unexpected difficulties beset the conqueror. The Burgundian king Gundobad, for example, sent an army into north Italy and laid waste the country. Theoderic had not only to drive these invaders out, but he had also to protect Sicily against the Vandals, who seized the opportunity of the war to attempt to recover it. Their attempt was frustrated, and they were forced to surrender the fortress of Lilybaeum as well as all their claims to the island.

It seems to have been in the same year that Theoderic resorted to a terrible measure for destroying the military garrisons which held Italian towns for Odovacar. The Italian population was generally favourable to the cause of Theoderic, and secret orders were given to the citizens to slaughter the soldiers on a prearranged day. The pious panegyrist, who exultantly, but briefly, describes this measure and claims Providence as an accomplice, designates it as a "sacrificial massacre"; and Theoderic doubtless considered that the treachery of his enemy's army in surrendering and then deserting justified an unusual act of vengeance. The secret of the plot was well kept, and it seems to have been punctually executed. The result was equivalent to another victory in the field; and nothing now remained for Theoderic but to capture the last stronghold of his adversary, the marsh city of Honorius.

The siege of Ravenna lasted for two years and a half. The Gothic forces entrenched themselves in a camp in the pine-woods east of the city, but were not able entirely to prevent provisions from reaching the garrison by sea. Yet the blockade was not ineffective, for corn rose to a famine price. One attempt was made by Odovacar to disperse the besiegers. He made a sortie at night (July 10, A.D. 491) with a band of Herul warriors and attacked the Gothic trenches. The conflict was obstinate; but he was defeated. Another year wore on, and it appeared that the siege might last for ever unless the food of the garrison could be completely cut off. Theoderic managed to procure a fleet of warships – we are not told whether or not they were built for the occasion – and, making the Portus Leonis, about six miles from Ravenna, his naval base, he was able to blockade the two harbours of the city (August A.D. 492). Odovacar held out for six months longer, but early in A.D. 493 negotiations, conducted by the bishop of Ravenna, issued in a compact between the two antagonists (February 25) that they should rule Italy jointly. Theoderic entered the city a week later (March 5).

The only way in which the compact could have been carried out would have been by a territorial division. But Theoderic had no mind to share the peninsula with another king, and there can hardly be a doubt that, when he swore to the treaty, he had the full intention of breaking his oath. Odovacar's days were numbered. Theoderic, a few days after his entry into Ravenna, slew him with his own hand in the palace of Laretum (March 15). He alleged that his defeated rival was plotting against him, but this probably was a mere pretext. "On the same day", adds the chronicler, "all Odovacar's soldiers were slain wherever they could be found, and all his kin."

In three years and a half Theoderic had accomplished his task. The reduction of Italy cost him four battles, a massacre, and a long siege. His capital blunder had been to trust Tufa after the victory of Verona. We may be sure that throughout the struggle he spared no pains to ingratiate himself in the confidence of the Italian population. But when his rival had fallen, and when he was at last securely established, Theoderic's first measure was to issue an edict depriving of their civil rights all those Italians who had not adhered to his cause. This harsh and stupid policy, however, was not carried out, for the bishop Epiphanius persuaded the king to revoke it and to promise that there would be no executions.

THE OSTROGOTHIC CONSTITUTION

The reign of Theoderic in Italy, if we date it from the battle of the Adda in 490, lasted thirty-six years, and it was, as I shall show, in its general principle, a continuation of the regime of Odovacar. Of Odovacar's government we know very little, of Theoderic's we know much; but the continuity is quite clear. One of the first things which Theoderic had to do was to settle his own people in the land, and this was done on exactly the same principle as the settlement of Odovacar. The Ostrogoths for the most part replaced Odovacar's Germans, who had been largely killed or driven out, though some of them embraced the rule of Theoderic and were permitted to remain in their lands. But the general principle was the assignment of one-third of the Roman estates to the Goths.

The Emperor Anastasius, who succeeded Zeno in 491, did not at first recognise Theoderic. But six years later they came to terms. In 497 a definite agreement was made; Anastasius recognised the position of Theoderic in Italy, subordinate to himself, on certain conditions. Then capitulation determined the constitutional position of Theoderic.

In order to understand the political aims of Theoderic, and his place as a statesman, it is indispensable to have a clear view of his constitutional position and the nature of his administration, and these matters will occupy the rest of this lecture. Fortunately there is very good material, for besides valuable notices in Procopius and a long fragment of an Italian chronicle, we have numerous state papers of Theoderic, drawn up by his state secretary, Cassiodorus.

The formal relation of Italy to the Empire, both under Odovacar and under Theoderic, was much closer and clearer than that of any other of the states ruled by Germans. Although practically independent, it was regarded officially both at Rome and at Constantinople as part of the Empire in the fullest sense. Two circumstances exhibit this theory very clearly. Odovacar and Theoderic never used the years of their own reigns for the purposes of dating, as the kings of the Visigoths did. Secondly, the right of naming one of the consuls of the year which had belonged to the emperor reigning in the west was transferred by the consent of the Emperors Zeno and Anastasius to Odovacar and Theoderic. So far as Theoderic is concerned, we have the express attestation of the historian Procopius; but Mommsen, who elucidated the whole subject, showed that the same principle applied to Odovacar. I may give a word of explanation as to the system of consular nomination in the fifth century. The rule was that the emperor reigning in the east and the emperor reigning in the west should each nominate one of the two men who were to be consuls for the one undivided Empire. But as a rule the two names were not published together. The name of the western consul was not known in the east, nor the name of the eastern in the west, in time for simultaneous publication. Hence the custom of successive publication. But there are exceptions. Between 421 and 530 there are twenty-three years in which the consular names were published together. Four of these are cases in which two emperors filled the consulship together, and as this was evidently done by prearrangement, the simultaneous publication is at once explained. But all the other cases, whether of two private persons or of an emperor and a private person, are peculiar. In more than half of them it is demonstrable that both consuls belonged to the same half of the Empire, whether east or west; thus in 437 both Aetius and Sigisvult belonged to the west: and of the other cases there is not a single one in which it can be shown that they belonged to different realms. We can infer with certainty that in these cases, one of the two nominators resigned his right in favour of the other, and that both consuls were nominated by the ruler of the half of the Empire to which they respectively belonged. This at once accounts for the simultaneous publication of the names. In the years 473 to 479 no consul was nominated in the west, owing to the unsettled conditions, but in 479 Zeno must have conceded to Odovacar the right of nominating a consul, for one of the consuls of 480, Basilius, almost certainly belonged to the west and was recognised in the east; and from this year we have a series of consuls appointed in the west up to the year of Odovacar's death, 493. This right did not immediately pass to Theoderic, because the Emperor Anastasius, Zeno's successor, did not immediately recognise him. From 494 to 497 the consular *fasti* exhibit exclusively eastern consuls. This shows Theoderic's tact. He would not widen his breach with the Emperor by assuming the right of naming a consul without his consent. But in 497 matters were arranged, and from 498 forward Theoderic named one of the consuls as Odovacar had done before him. In 522 the Emperor Justin waived his own nomination and allowed Theoderic to name both consuls – Symmachus and Boethius. It would be interesting to know whether this exceptional favour had anything to do with the anti-German and anti-Arian sentiments of these two patricians which brought about their fall.

There was one limitation which Theoderic recognised in this matter: he could not nominate a Goth; only Romans could fill the consulship, and indeed only Romans could fill the other magistracies. The rule is corroborated by the single exception: in 519 Eutharic, Theoderic's son-in-law, was consul. But it is expressly recorded that this nomination was not made by Theoderic; it was made by the Emperor. This shows that in the capitulations of Theoderic to the government of Constantinople, one article was that a Goth should not fill the consulship. And so when Theoderic desired an exception in favour of his son-in-law, the favour had to come from the Emperor.

The capitulation which excluded Goths from the consulship extended also to all the civil offices, which were maintained under Ostrogothic rule, as they had been under Odovacar's. There was still the praetorian prefect of Italy, and when Theoderic acquired Provence the office of Praetorian Prefect of Gaul was revived. There was the *vicarius urbis Romae* , as before. There were all the provincial governors, divided as before into the three ranks of *consulares, correctores* , and *praesides* . There were the two finance officers, the *comes sacrarum largitionum* and the *comes rerum privatarum* . Anastasius instituted a new financial officer, the *comes patrimonii* , who shared the functions of the *comes rerum privatarum* , and Theoderic followed his example. But in this case he did not conform to the rule which excluded Goths; several of his *comites patrimonii* have German names; the office does not seem to have been regarded as a regular state office; or perhaps it was treated as an exception because it was instituted after the capitulation had been made. All the *officia* , or staffs of subordinate officials, were maintained under Theoderic's regime. In the state documents we often read of *officium nostrum* ; that means the bureau of the *magister officiorum* , who was the chief commander of the *scholae* of bodyguards and was at the head of all the subordinate officials of the palace. Both the praetorian prefect and the *magister officiorum* reside at Ravenna, but they have each a representative at Rome, who belongs to the same rank of illustres as themselves. The drafting of state documents, the official correspondence of the king, was carried on by the *quaestor palatii* , an office which was long filled by Cassiodorus. It may be added that the exclusion of Goths also applied to the honorary title of Patricius. Under Theoderic no Goth bore that title but Theoderic himself, who had received it from the Emperor.

But if Goths were excluded from the civil posts, it was exactly the reverse in the case of the military posts. Here it was the Romans who were excluded. The army was entirely Gothic; no Roman was liable to military service; and the officers were naturally Goths. The regiments are formed by the Goths settled in the districts of the various towns. In consequence of the confiscation of one-third of the land for the Gothic freemen, every territory in the peninsula ought to have had a garrison of these settlers; but as a matter of fact the settlements were not uniformly distributed, and the Gothic population in the south of the peninsula did not amount to much. We know practically nothing about the organisation of the army; but it seems likely that each territory in which Goths were settled had to supply men in proportion to the number of acres. The chief officers were called *priors* or *counts* . But although the old Roman troops and their organisation have disappeared (in consequence of the exclusion of Romans), it has been shown by Mommsen that the military arrangements of Theoderic were based in many respects on arrangements which had existed in Italy under imperial rule in the fifth century. Now what about the highest office of all, that of Master of Soldiers? Under Odovacar we hear of Masters of Soldiers. But under Ostrogothic rule no Master of Soldiers is mentioned. The generals employed by Theoderic are not described by this title. In the long list of the *formulae* of the various offices which existed in Italy at this time the Mastership of the Soldiers does not appear, and that cannot be explained as an oversight.

Yet the office had not ceased to exist; for we find in a letter of Cassiodorus the mention of an *officialis magistri militum* , 'a subaltern of the Master of Soldiers'. The solution, as Mommsen has shown, is that Theoderic himself was the *magister militum* . He had, as we saw, received that title – *magister militum praesentalis* – from Zeno ten years before he conquered Italy; he bore it when he conquered Italy, and he continued to retain it while he ruled Italy. It is intelligible that he did not designate himself by this title, because his powers as ruler of Italy far exceeded the powers of the most powerful *magister militum* ; but this does not nean that he gave the office up. It explains why the title was never given to any of his generals. The matter is illustrated by certain measures taken after Theoderic's death. His grandson and successor, the vicious lad Athalaric, was out of the question as commander of the forces, and his mother, Amalasuntha, who acted as regent, appointed a Gothic warrior, Tuluin, and Liberius, a Roman, who was the Praetorian Prefect of Gaul, to be *patricii praesentales* . This remarkable appointment involved two deviations from existing rules. It gave the rank of Patricius to Tuluin, who as a Goth was excluded from that title; and it gave a military command to Liberius, who as a Roman was incapable of such. The office, though under this modified title, was simply that of *magister militum praesentalis* , but the circumstance that the title was modified is significant, and illustrates the fact that the office of magister militum had become closely united to that of king, through the long tenure of it by Theoderic.

It need hardly be said that as the Goths were excluded from civil offices, so they were excluded from the Roman senate. The senate continued to exist under the Ostrogothic kings, and to perform the same functions as it had performed throughout the fifth century. It was still formally recognised as a sovran body. Theoderic writes: *parem nobiscum reipublicae debetis adnisum* . The senate like the emperor could *leges constituere* , and the constitutional difference between a senator and the emperor was that the senator was under the law and the emperor was not. But only the senators of the highest class, the *illustres* , had the right of voting, and as this class consisted of men who held the highest state offices, and were appointed by the emperor, it was the emperor who nominated the senators. Such was the constitutional position of the senate: politically it had no power, and its functions were practically confined to the affairs of Rome.

The position of Theoderic as deputy-governor of the emperor, and the position of Italy as part of the empire is shown by the maintenance of the imperial sovran rights in coinage and in legislation. Theoderic did not claim the right of coining except in subordination to the emperor. The silver coins of his reign show the Emperor Anastasius (*dominus noster Anastasius*) on the obverse, and on the reverse Theoderic's monogram with the legend *invicta Roma* . Did he claim the right of making laws? In Procopius, it is expressly stated by representatives of the Goths, that neither Theoderic nor any of the Gothic rulers issued a law. This statement involves the admission that the right of legislation was the supreme prerogative of the emperor. And there is no formal contradiction between this statement and the fact that ordinances of Theoderic exist. None of these ordinances are designated as *leges* . They are only *edicta* . The *lex* , and the making of a *lex* , was the exclusive right of the emperor; but various high officials could issue an *edictum* . Here then, formally, the regime of Theoderic stands in marked contrast with the regime in the western kingdoms which did not depend on Constantinople. The Ostrogothic king issues edicts, the contemporary Burgundian king enacts *leges, mansurae in aevum leges* .

But was this difference between the law and the edict, between the right of the emperor and the right of the king, merely a formal one? Did it mean no more than the difference of a name, that Theoderic called his laws *edicta* , while the laws of Anastasius or Justin were *leges* ? Theoderic certainly promulgated what Cassiodorus calls *edicta generalia* , laws which did not concern special cases, but were of a general kind permanently valid, and which, if they had been enacted by the emperor, would have been called *leges* . But it must be remembered that the highest officials of the empire, especially the praetorian prefect, had the right of issuing an *edictum generate, provided it did not run counter to any existing law* . This may sound like a contradiction, but practically it was a very important distinction. It amounted to this, that the praetorian prefect could modify existing laws, in subordinate points, whether in the direction of mildness or severity or definition, but could not originate any new principle or institution. Now the ordinances of Theoderic which are collected in his code, known as the *Edictum Theoderici* , exhibit conformity to this rule. They introduce no new institutions; they alter no established principle. When he first appeared in Rome we are told that Theoderic addressed the people and promised that he would preserve inviolate *omnia quod retro principes ordinaverunt* . Procopius twice emphasises the fact that he preserved the laws of the empire. Theoderic himself, through the official mouthpiece of Cassiodorus, repeatedly dwells on this principle of the regime: "*nescimus a legibus discrepare* "; "*sufficiens laus conscientiae est veterum decreta servare* ". Thus in the matter of legislation the king is neither nominally nor really co-ordinate with the emperor. His legislative powers are those of a great official, such as a praetorian prefect, and though he employed these powers to a greater extent than any praetorian prefect could have done, owing to the circumstances of the case, yet his edicts are qualitatively on the same footing, and are qualitatively quite distinct from the laws which the emperor might make. In legislation, the position of Theoderic as an official of the empire is clear and unmistakable, and it is remarkable how loyally he adhered to the capitulations.

It is important to have a clear idea of the legal position of the Goths in Italy. The Goths settled by Theoderic, like the Germans settled by Odovacar, had legally exactly the same status as mercenaries, or travellers, or hostages who dwelled on Roman territory, but might at any time return to their homes beyond the Roman frontier. The fact that these Germans had made their homes on Roman soil, though it altered practically their position, did not alter their legal status. They were foreign soldiers, without Roman citizenship. But you must observe that this by no means implies that Roman law did not apply to them. We have to distinguish between the laws which have a territorial and those which have a personal application. To the former class belong all laws pertaining to criminal matters and to the general intercourse of life, and these were applicable to all foreigners who happened to be sojourning in Roman territory. The personal laws, which concerned only Roman citizens, were mainly those which related to marriage and inheritance. These had no application to foreigners, and one consequence was that if a foreigner died on Roman soil his property fell to the state as unowned property, there being no legal heir, the laws of inheritance not applying to him. This was the condition of the Gothic soldiers in Italy. They were not Roman citizens: Theoderic speaks of a certain Goth, who had acquired Roman culture, as *civis paene vester* , 'almost a Roman citizen'. The only Goth in Italy who possessed Roman citizenship was Theoderic himself. The Goths did not belong to any municipal community. They were not even *incolae* . When a citizen of Naples went to live at Beneventum, he became an *incola* of Beneventum; but a foreigner, a Moor or a Frank, did not become an *incola* of the place where he lived, and neither did the Goth. And here we touch on another important restriction of Theoderic's powers. He could not turn a Goth into a Roman; he could not bestow Roman citizenship; that power was reserved for the Emperor.

The Goths then were foreign soldiers. Their quality as soldiers determined the character of the courts in which they were judged. The Roman rule at this time was that the soldier could be tried by a military court only, and Theoderic instituted military courts for the Goths on this principle. But here we come to a serious and important interference on the part of Theoderic with the rights of the Romans. All processes between Goths and Romans, to whichever race the accuser belonged, were brought before these military courts. In such cases a Roman lawyer was always present as an assessor; but probably no feature of the Gothic regime was so unpopular as this. So far as the *personal* law was concerned, the Goths and Romans lived side by side, each according to their own laws. But – and this is a very important fact – the *territorial* law, criminal jurisprudence and laws affecting general intercourse, applied to the Goths as well as to the Romans: this was the *jus commune* of which Theoderic speaks, and his Edict, which is based on Roman law, is addressed to Goths and Romans indiscriminately.

Theoderic, like the emperor, had a supreme royal court, which could withdraw any case from a lower court, or cancel its decision; and this court seems to have been much more active than the corresponding court of the emperor. It is indeed in the domain of justice, in striking contrast with the domain of legislation, that the German kings in Italy asserted their actual authority.

Besides holding the Roman office of *magister militum* in regard to the foreign soldiers, Theoderic was likewise their king. I have already called your attention to the fact that Theoderic was originally not king of the whole Ostrogothic people, but only a *gaukönig* , one among other Ostrogothic kings. On the conquest of Italy, the extent of his kingly power, that is the number of his subjects, increased through the circumstance that those of Odovacar's German settlers whom he did not extirpate or banish acknowledged him as their king; this was notably the case with the Rugians. His position in Italy then in regard to the foreign settlers is that of a German king; but those settlers are not all Ostrogoths. As a matter of fact Theoderic did not call himself "king of the Goths": he designated his position by the Latin title *rex* , but he never called himself *rex Gotorum* . But his adoption of this style, *rex* , his avoidance of *rex Gotorum* , was certainly not influenced by the fact that his German subjects embraced a larger circle than the Ostrogoths whom he had led to conquer Italy. It was rather due to his relation to the Roman population. For although *formally and constitutionally* the Roman citizens of Italy were the subjects of the emperor, of whom Theoderic himself was a subject and official, yet actually and politically they were in the hands of Theoderic, who was their ruler. This actual relation of Theoderic to the Roman population was unconstitutional, or perhaps I should say extra-constitutional, and there was no constitutional term to designate it. Theoderic used the word *rex* to signify this unwritten relation; for remember that *rex* had no constitutional meaning in the empire, no place in the vocabulary of the imperial constitution. It was an extremely convenient term, when used thus without any closer definition, to designate at once his regular relation to his German subjects, and his irregular relation, his quasi-kingship, to the Romans of Italy. If he had called himself *rex Gotorum* , he would thereby have seemed to exclude the Romans from that higher authority which he possessed beyond the power of an ordinary imperial official. On the other hand, it would have been impossible for him to describe himself as *rex Gotorum et Romanorum* , for *rex Romanorum* would have been a glaring unconstitutional monstrosity. The simple and vague *rex* was the most appropriate term to suggest that actual sovran authority which he exercised over the German settlers and Roman citizens alike.

But this title, this style, *was not the invention of Theoderic* . It was the usage of his predecessor Odovacar, and was clearly taken over by Theoderic from him. Fortunately we possess one original official document from the chancery of Odovacar. It is a deed of gift, written on papyrus, and is preserved in two fragments, of which one is at Vienna and the other at Naples. Odovacar grants therein some farms at Syracuse to Pierius the Count of Domestics. The important point is that Odovacar is here officially designated as *rex* . The Ostrogothic dynasty adopted this style. And this is a noteworthy fact, because it is part of a larger fact which has not been sufficiently recognised and which I want to impress upon you, that in regard to the constitutional principle and the administrative system the Ostrogothic regime is simply a continuation of the regime of Odovacar: there is no break; the substitution of Theoderic is from this point of view simply a change of person. The historian who has most fully recognised this fact is Heinrich von Sybel. Everything points to the assumption that the capitulations of the agreement between Theoderic and Anastasius corresponded in all essential points to the arrangement which Odovacar had made with Zeno. And I think it is not unimportant to observe a circumstance which helped to secure and facilitate administrative continuity. The first Praetorian Prefect of Italy under Theoderic's government was Liberius, who held the office for seven years from A.D. 493 to 500. Now this Liberius was one of the chief ministers of Odovacar, though we do not know what post he held. He supported his first master loyally until the final catastrophe, and he transferred his services to Theoderic, who wisely accepted them. Another minister of

Odovacar was Cassiodorus – not the famous Cassiodorus whose writings are our chief authority for the Ostrogothic period, but his father. Cassiodorus, the father, was a finance minister under Odovacar. He had held both of the great financial offices; he had been Count of the Sacred Largess, and Count of the Private Estate. He stood aloof apparently in the contest between Theoderic and Odovacar; and when that contest was decided, he served under Theoderic, and in the early years of the sixth century became praetorian prefect. To return to my point: Liberius and Cassiodorus were two conspicuous instances in which the ministers of Odovacar's regime continued to take part in Theoderic's administration; and there were doubtless a great many cases of the kind. This continuity of the personnel of the civil service is significant, because it helped to secure Italy against breach or change in the administration.

I have tried to bring out the thoroughly Roman character of the Italian kingdom. The question will naturally be asked: How far did Germanic influences make themselves felt in Theoderic's administration? In the first place, of course, as I have already noted, the Germans lived, so far as their own *personal* relations were concerned, according to Germanic laws and customs. But in the general administration there are one or two cases where Germanic influence may have operated. Let us take the case of the officer called by the Gothic name of *saio* , who was always a Goth. These officers were marshals or messengers whom the king employed to intimate his commands. They were employed to summon the Gothic soldiers to arms, or to call a Roman official to a sense of duty. If a praetorian prefect attempted an act of oppression, Theoderic sent a *saio* to inform him that this kind of thing could not be allowed. Now, the office of *saio* may well represent a German institution. But it is well to insist on the fact that it *can be explained* without that assumption; there need be nothing Gothic about it but the name. For there were other officers who were called by a Roman name and had exactly similar functions. There were the *comitiaci* who were subordinate to the *magister officiorum* . Mommsen has shown that these *comitiaci* are identical with the well-known *agentes in rebus* , one whose duties was to execute special missions of the Emperor. Thus the *saiones* may merely represent a transference to the Goths of a Roman institution.

There is another institution which we find active under Theoderic, and in which I think a certain Germanic influence may have been at work. This is the *tuitio* . It is a purely Roman institution in itself. The earliest mention we have of it is in a law of A.D. 393. Any person who considered his personal safety in danger might apply for special protection, and a judge was bound to assign an officer to assist and protect him. The officer must not be a soldier, but a civil officer – an *apparitor* . Whether the Emperor ever himself granted a *tuitio* of this kind we do not know; no case is recorded, and we may assume that he was seldom or never called upon to do so. Such petitions cannot, in the ordinary course of things, have come before the highest court of all. Now this practice of *tuitio* plays a very prominent part in Ostrogothic Italy, and we find it mainly as a protection granted by the king himself. It was one of the methods by which the king preserved peace and order among the two races; it was used to protect Roman against Goth and Goth against Roman. A Roman proprietor who felt his life or property threatened by an aggressive Gothic neighbour could apply to the royal court for an officer to protect him, and a *saio* would be quartered in his house for that purpose. Now it seems highly probable that the quickening of this Roman custom under the Gothic government, and its special association with the king himself, may have been partly due to the influence of the Germanic idea of the king's duty of protection, the *Königsschutz* – an idea which was very important among the Franks. The old German word for it was *Munt* , now obsolete, but preserved in some compounds like *Vormund* , 'guardian', and *unmündig* , 'under age.'

THE REIGN OF THEODERIC

We have considered the regime of Theoderic from the constitutional point of view – as founded upon the capitulations agreed upon between him and the emperor. We have seen how sharply it was distinguished in this respect from the position of the other German kingdoms in the west, when they were first founded. We must now regard it briefly from a political point of view. The essential fact is that the constitutional system of administration which Theoderic adopted and observed was not a necessity to which he reluctantly or half-heartedly yielded; it was a system in which he was a convinced believer, and into the working of which he threw his whole heart and his best energies. His avowed political object was to civilise his own people in the environment of Roman civilisation. The circumstance that Roman law was applicable, under his government, to the Goths in Italy, just as far as it was applicable to *peregrini* in any part of the Empire, was an important condition in furthering this object. But Theoderic made no premature attempt to draw the two classes of his subjects nearer, by breaking down lines of division. They were divided from one another in two ways, by religion and by legal status – just as in the Visigothic kingdom. So far as religion was concerned, Theoderic was ardently tolerant, his principle was "*Religionem imperare non possumus quia nemo cogitur ut credat invitus* ": we cannot command religion because no one can be compelled to believe against his will. So extreme was his repugnance to influencing the religion of his fellow-creatures, that an anecdote was invented that he put to death a Catholic deacon for embracing Arianism in order to please him. If there is any truth in the tale, there must have been other circumstances; but in any case it is evidence for Theoderic's religious attitude, for if it was entirely invented it illustrates his reputation. The only people whom Theoderic desired to convert were the Jews; but to them also he extended in fullest measure his policy of toleration.

And just as he accepted the duality of religion, he accepted and maintained the dual system of Goth and Roman as two distinct and separate peoples living side by side. He accepted the government of this double population as the problem which he had to solve; he took no steps to bring about fusion; his only aim was that the two nations should live together in amity. It might be asked how far he regarded this state of things as no more than a stage; whether he thought that a day would come when the Gothic *peregrini* , assimilated by their Roman neighbours, would be admitted to Roman citizenship and intermarriage; whether he looked forward to a fusion of the two races in the future. To such a question I think we may answer, probably, No. He did not look beyond the dual system, nor comprehend that the dual system could not be permanent. The Ostrogothic kingdom was overthrown before such a fusion could begin. But the development in the Visigothic kingdom, under similar conditions, suggests that some fusion would have ensued, if the Ostrogothic kingdom had endured.

In foreign politics Theoderic acted as an independent sovran, and his great aim here corresponded to his aim in his own kingdom. As his object in Italy was to maintain law and order, what he called *civilitas* , so on the wider scene of Western Europe his object was to maintain peace and the existing order of things. The four chief powers which came into account were the Visigoths, the Vandals, the Burgundians, and the Franks. It was natural that Theoderic should look for special co-operation from the Visigoths, who besides being Arian were a kindred folk. But his policy was not to form a close, intimate alliance with the Visigoths, which could only seem a threat and a danger to the other powers. He sought to form bonds of friendship and alliance with all the reigning houses. If he wedded one of his daughters to Alaric, king of the Visigoths, the other married Sigismund, who became king of the Burgundians after his father Gundobad's death. Theoderic himself took as his second wife a Frankish princess, sister of Clovis. Moreover, his own sister married Thrasamund, king of the Vandals. Thus he formed close ties by marriage with all the chief powers of the west. In addition, his niece married a king of the Thuringians.

The character and spirit of Theoderic's policy are exhibited in his intervention in favour of the Alamanni. This people, after their defeat by Clovis, had moved southward into Baden,

Würtemburg, and eastern Switzerland. Some years later Clovis decided to pursue them and extirpate them. Theoderic wrote to his brother-in-law advising him not to push his victory further. "Hear the counsel of one who has experience in such matters. Those wars of mine have been successful the ending of which has been guided by moderation." The Alamanni were taken under the protection of Theoderic, being settled in the province of Rhaetia, which officially belonged to Italy; and they served there as a sort of frontier garrison.

But the family alliances of Theoderic did not avail to hinder war or to prevent the inevitable struggle between the Franks and Visigoths in Gaul. No moment in his reign perhaps caused more anxiety and vexation than when Clovis declared war against Alaric. He did all he could to avert it. We have the three letters he wrote at this crisis to Alaric, to Gundobad, and to Clovis himself. It was in vain. But the remarkable thing is that Theoderic did not render the help which he promised to his son-in-law Alaric. The probability seems to be that he had not calculated upon the Burgundians taking the side of the Franks, and that they cut him off in 507 from marching to Aquitaine in time to intervene in the struggle. But in 508 and the next two years his generals conducted campaigns in Gaul, and succeeded in rescuing the city of Arles and in saving Narbonensis for the Visigoths. These campaigns resulted also in an acquisition for Theoderic himself. Provence was wrested from the Burgundians and annexed to Italy. The power of Theoderic also received another extension. The heir of Alaric, who had fallen in the battle of Vouille, was a child. The government of Spain was consigned to Theoderic, who was the boy's grandfather and his most powerful protector; and for the rest of his life he ruled Spain in his own name. He ruled it quite independently, and the union in the same hands of Spain, the independent kingdom, and Italy, the imperial dependency, exhibits in a striking way the contrast between them.

Theoderic died in 526, and within ten years from his death the struggle began which ended in the destruction of his work, the overthrow of the Ostrogothic kingdom. The stage was cleared for a new development. It may then seem unnecessary to have dwelt at such comparative length on the reign of Theoderic and the Ostrogothic period, seeing that it was an episode which led to nothing and had no morrow. But the importance of studying the Ostrogothic regime is not so much due to its place in the development of events, as to the light it throws, both by way of similarity and by way of contrast, on the process of the formation and on the conditions of the kingdoms into which the western half of the Empire broke up. It helps us to understand the position of the Visigothic federate kingdom and the Burgundian federate kingdom in Gaul when they were first planted; it helps us to understand how the parallel dual systems worked in other lands; it helps us to realise the problems of government which the other German kings had to solve, whether they were still federate or had ceased to be federate; it helps us to apprehend the attitude and aims of the half-Romanised Germans.

I cannot include the story of the fall of the Ostrogothic kingdom, and the resumption of Italy under the immediate government of the emperor, within the compass of these lectures. I have only to remind you that Justinian's conquest of Africa and his conquest of Italy differed in one important point. In the case of Africa, he was recovering lost provinces from a power which was quite independent of the Empire. In the case of Italy, he was resuming the direct government of a territory which had been committed to the sway of a regent who in theory fully acknowledged the imperial authority and accepted the limitations which had been laid down by that authority. Observe also that to the Roman population of Italy the change of masters was welcome; the Goths were still aliens to them, and they were heretical aliens as well. This difference in religion was of fundamental importance.

The fall of the Ostrogothic kingdom reminds us of the comparative failure of the East German peoples to perform their early promise. It had seemed, a century earlier, that the fate of western Europe lay with them. The Vandal and the Ostrogothic kingdoms had now both disappeared. The Visigothic still survived, but at the beginning of the eighth century it was to go down before invaders from Asia. It was the only one of the three which was to have abiding effect on the country in which it was established. The fourth, the Burgundian, had already been absorbed into the Merovingian realm. Two of the sons of Clovis conquered it in 532. But it maintained an integral identity of its own within that realm; an identity which was marked by the continued use of Burgundian law.

Lecture 12:
Visigoths and Franks in Gaul

THE KINGDOM OF TOULOUSE UNDER EURIC – THE ROMAN REMNANT IN GAUL – THE EARLY HISTORY OF THE FRANKS – THE REIGN OF CHILDERIC THE FRANK

THE KINGDOM OF TOULOUSE UNDER EURIC

We must now turn from Italy to observe how the power of the barbarians had been advancing in the provinces farther west. The great growth of the Visigothic kingdom, the kingdom of Toulouse, as it was called, belongs to the time of Euric. This powerful king, son of that Theodoric who had perished in the great battle against Attila in 451, was the third of three brothers – Thorismund, Theodoric II., Euric – to ascend the Visigothic throne. He gained the throne by murdering his predecessor in 466, and he reigned till 484. He was probably the greatest of the Visigothic kings. Not only did he show conspicuous ability both in war and diplomacy, but he was also the first of the Visigothic legislators. He not only succeeded in achieving those territorial acquisitions for the kingdom which his predecessors had in vain attempted to make, but he extended the realm far beyond the bounds at which they had aimed. In Gaul he carried his frontier to the Loire and to the Rhone. A few years before his accession the Visigoths had won Narbonensis, including Narbonne but not including Arles; they acquired thereby a sea-board on the Mediterranean. Euric gained possession of Arles and Marseilles, and in 481, after the death of the Emperor Julius Nepos, the whole of Provence to the border of Italy was formally conceded to him by Odovacar, who professed to represent the imperial authority. Meantime, Euric had advanced northwards, and had won the province of Aquitania Prima, which stretched from Orleans to Vienne, and included the district of Auvergne. This district held out longest against the Visigoths, and the fierceness of the struggle of the Roman magnates against the Goths is reflected in the pages of the poet and bishop Sidonius Apollinaris,

But Euric was no less active in Spain than in Gaul. His predecessors had constantly made incursions into Spain against the Suevians, and had generally cooperated with the Romans. In fact, in these Spanish wars they might be considered as continuing the work of Wallia, as imperial federates, helping to protect Roman Spain against the Suevians. Euric continued the war against the Suevians; but it carried him much farther. He not only conquered a part of Suevic territory, but he extended his power ultimately over the whole of Roman Spain, except a few strong places on the coast. We may say that by the year 478, all Spain, except the north-western corner where the disabled and weakened Suevian kingdom continued to exist, had been incorporated in the Visigothic kingdom. By the year 481 Euric's dominion stretched from the Straits to the Loire. In Gaul it was bounded by the Atlantic, the Loire, and the Rhone, with the addition of Provence, east of the Rhone. It was now at the height of its territorial power, and it seemed in these years, from 480 onwards, far the greatest and most promising state of western Europe. In fact, anyone surveying western Europe at that moment could hardly have failed to conclude that its destinies depended on the Visigoths.

THE ROMAN REMNANT IN GAUL

The Roman power, however, had not yet wholly disappeared. I must go back to say that after the death of Aetius, in 454, the great bulwark of the imperial authority had been Aegidius, a native of western Gaul. For ten years, doubtless as *magister militum* , he had maintained the frontiers with varying success against the Visigoths; as to his relations with the Franks I shall have to speak later on. After his death about 464 or 465, the defence of the Gallo-Romans devolved upon his son Syagrius, who was unable to resist the advance of Euric to the Loire. But he maintained the north of Gaul, the lands of the Seine and Somme against the Goths on the south, and against the Franks on the east. The position was difficult, and it was mainly by keeping on good terms with the Franks that Aegidius had been able to maintain it. It seemed probable that the Gothic power would soon advance to the Channel, and that the remnant of Roman provincial government would be crushed out. Indeed, it actually was crushed out in a few years, but not, as everyone might have expected, by the Goths. It was crushed out by the Franks, after Euric's death, an event the treatment of which belongs to another lecture. But I would insist here on the great prospect which to all outward appearance the Visigothic kingdom possessed during the last four years of Euric's reign, 480-484. The Goths seemed almost certain to be the ultimate inheritors of all Gaul, and they had already acquired almost all Spain. It is interesting to realise this apparent probability, which the actual course of things so markedly belied.

I think it is likely that the subjugation of all Gaul was a dream which Euric dreamed, and hoped to realise. His policy is thus expressed by Jordanes, who was no doubt copying Cassiodorus: "Euric saw the frequent change of Roman Emperors and the tottering state of the Empire: so he determined to be independent and to subdue Gaul." This general statement of Euric's policy is borne out by the facts; he made very considerable steps towards carrying it out. It is possible that if he had lived longer he might have done more. But I do not believe that he or any other king of the Visigoths, however able, could have accomplished Euric's dream unless they had fulfilled one condition. I come here to what was probably the principal and radical cause of the remarkable failure of the Visigoths, notwithstanding their splendid promise. It was their religion; they were Arians. If Euric or his son Alaric had embraced the Catholic creed and brought about the conversion of his people, the course of history in Gaul might have been quite different. The weak joint in the armour of the Visigothic kings was the antagonism of the Roman population and their clergy to their heretical rulers. This cause of weakness was not confined to the Visigoths: it appears with similar effects in the case of the other great East German kingdoms. I think it is not too much to lay down the general proposition that the Arian heresy was one main cause of the striking fact that the East German peoples who had begun so brilliantly, sweeping, as it were, all before them, ended their career in failure. The three leading cases are the Vandals, the Visigoths, and the Ostrogoths. The overthrow of the Vandal kingdom by the forces of the Empire might never have been achieved but for the fanatical devotion of the Vandals to their heretical creed and their persecution of the Catholic provincials. It was the same with the still shorter lived Ostrogothic kingdom in Italy; for, although the Ostrogoths did not persecute, their rule could never establish itself on a popular basis because they were Arians; and it was the difference in faith, keeping the Goths and the Italians apart, and the rallying of the Italians to the side of an orthodox conqueror, that conduced above all to the success of the imperialist armies which reconquered Italy under Justinian. The Visigothic kingdom did not come to an untimely end like the Vandal and the Ostrogothic; yet it not only fell short of the success which it seemed likely to achieve, but it did collapse suddenly in Gaul. But before we consider that collapse we must follow the history of the Franks.

THE EARLY HISTORY OF THE FRANKS

The united strength of Roman and Goth had repulsed the Hun from Gaul, but neither Roman emperor nor Gothic king was destined permanently to inherit it. We have now to trace the rise of the power of the Franks, who in less than sixty years after the deaths of King Theodoric I. (451) and Aetius (454) had annexed the territory of Roman and Visigoth alike. Considering their importance, considering the fact that contemporary chroniclers were still recording events in the fifth century in Gaul, our knowledge of the rise and advance of the Salian Franks is curiously meagre. Our chief authority is the *Historia Francorum* of Gregory of Tours, the historian who is for the Franks what Cassiodorus is for the Goths, Bede for the Anglo-Saxons, Paul the Deacon for the Lombards. Gregory wrote towards the end of the sixth century, and brought his history down to his own time. From 561 to 591 – the year with which his story terminates – for these thirty years he narrates events of which he was contemporary. But up to 561, from the beginning of the fifth century, his sketch of the history of the Franks is derived from sources the nature of which we are only just beginning to understand. As everything depends on Gregory of Tours, I must begin by explaining briefly his method and the value of his material. He had no Roman historians to help him. He does, it is true, at the very outset find something to his purpose in Sulpicius Severus and in Renatus Frigeridus Profuturus; but of these the former stops before the end of the fourth century, while Renatus does not come down very far into the fifth, and stops before the serious advance of the Franks begins. In the fifth century, annals take the place of histories in the Latin half of the Empire, and Gregory got what he could out of the annals which were accessible to him. Besides the annals he was able to get some information from Lives of Saints, and we find him using the *Life of St. Remigius*. But beyond these we may say with certainty that he had no written sources.

Like all the other German peoples, the Franks had their heroic songs, and these songs were not only about the remote past; they celebrated living or recently dead chieftains, together with recent and contemporary events. Historical facts were altered by popular imagination, and gradually cast into legendary moulds which conformed them to the spirit of epic poetry. The existence of poetry of this kind can be proved among all the chief German peoples. That the character and origin of these narratives have been so slowly recognised is due to the semi-critical attitude of Gregory in receiving and recording them. He did not know the Frank tongue himself, and he must have got friends who knew the songs to tell him the gist of them. He evidently distrusted these Frank traditions, but he had no other source, and was obliged to make use of them. But he shows his distrust and contempt for them, as compared with written sources, by never designating them, or referring to them by any more particular formula than *ut ferunt* , or the like. He mentions his *written* authorities because he regarded a written authority as a guarantee of correctness; but he had little respect for popular rumour or tradition, and did not consider it a guarantee at all. This is the characteristic sceptical attitude of the Roman man of letters to oral tradition. You understand, then, that the Franks of Gregory's time had their heroic songs not only of the remote past, but also of the very recent past; and that the popular imagination was still busy in Gregory's own day with the invention of new works of poetical creation.

Let us see what we can make out of this material concerning the early history of the Franks. The first Salian king of whom Gregory of Tours tells us is Chlodio, and here too it can be shown that he gained his information not from any written sources, but from the traditions, the poetical traditions, of the Franks. I may quote verbally his notice of Chlodio: it is highly important. "It is related that Chlodio, a brave man and the most noble of his race, was at that time king of the Franks. He lived in the stronghold of Dispargum, which is in the borders of the Thuringians. Chlodio sent reconnoitrers to the city of Cameracum (Cambrai): they explored the whole district, and then Chlodio followed, defeated the Romans and captured the city, where he resided for some time. Then he occupied all the country as far as the river Somme." This notice is a brief summary of the drift of a Frankish tale of which Chlodio was the hero. You observe here the land of the Thuringians means a land west of the lower Rhine on the north-east border of France. You observe too how Gregory is, in spite of himself, under the influence of his source. In such a brief notice he might better have left out the details of the sending forth of reconnoitrers and the king himself following subsequently; we ought either to have more details or none at all. Fortunately for us he has left them in; for they indicate clearly, as Kurth has pointed out, that he was abbreviating from a much fuller story in which those details had interest and significance.

The stronghold of Dispargum is, no doubt, historical; we need not doubt that it was a stronghold north of the great forest, the Silva Carbonaria, which bounded the Frankish territory on the south. But what about Chlodio himself? Is he a historical person or a legendary figure? If we had no evidence but this notice of Gregory of Tours we might feel considerable doubt as to his reality. But by a lucky chance we have another piece of evidence which completely reassures us that Chlodio was a real king of the Franks, and one, moreover, which gives us a chronological date. This important testimony is found in a poem of Sidonius Apollinaris. The poet describes an episode in the career of the great Roman general Aetius, his own contemporary. He tells how Chlodio with his Franks invaded the plains of Artois. He encamped near a place called Vicus Helena, and his warriors, deeming themselves quite secure, celebrated the wedding of one of their comrades. As they are engaged in songs and festivity, Aetius is suddenly seen on the road descending into the valley. The Franks, taken unprepared, are routed, and the bride and bridegroom fall into the hands of the conquerors. This precious text assures us, in the first place, of the reality of King Chlodio; in the second place, it shows us that the Frank tradition is historically correct in representing Chlodio as trying to extend his dominion in the direction of Artois; in the third place, it gives us a date for King Chlodio's reign, since the incident recorded by Sidonius can be fixed to the year A.D. 431 or thereabouts. But how very instructive the existence of this testimony is! Sidonius was not a historian; and it was only a chance that he should have chosen to tell this story. If he had not told the story, the existence of Chlodio would have been a subject for legitimate doubt. It is a most useful warning to us, that tradition must be criticised and not merely set aside.

In the present case, Sidonius also furnishes a valuable clue for criticising the record of the Frank tradition. In the account of Gregory, Chlodio first seizes Cambrai, which implies that he penetrated through the Carbonarian forest, and then proceeds to reduce all the land as far as the Somme. These achievements are conceived in this tradition as a single great successful expedition. That this conception was not historical is shown by the story in Sidonius, from which we learn that the able Roman general was in the field against the Franks, and that he drove them back. We must therefore conclude that the conquests of Chlodio, if they did finally reach to the Somme, were achieved slowly and not in one glorious advance. That the national song should have pressed into a single enterprise events that were scattered over years is perfectly natural.

We have now *two fixed points* in the advance of the Franks; 358 for their advance from the island of Batavia into Flanders, and 430-431 for their next advance southward in the direction of the Somme. After this we lose sight of them again until the invasion of Gaul by the Huns in 451. At that crisis, as we saw, the Salians embraced the cause of Rome. They were still, of course, regarded as part of the Empire, living within its borders, and nominally subjects of the emperors. But we are not told who was king of the Salian Franks at the battle of the Mauriac plain. Now, according to the Frankish tradition as recorded by Gregory, King Chlodio was succeeded by Merovech or Meroveus, and Merovech by Childeric. About Childeric there is no difficulty or doubt; we know that he was already king in A.D. 457. But the intervening Merovech is surrounded by mystery. Our only definite notices of him are derived from Frank legend, and they hint at some curious secret about his origin. Gregory of Tours has no doubt about his existence; but he was in doubt about his birth. He says mysteriously "*Some believe* that Meroveus is of the seed of Chlodio"; but he does not mention any rival theory. Clearly he wished to believe that Merovech was Chlodio's son: but the Frank tradition raised such doubts that he felt himself unable to speak positively. Fredegarius teaches us what the legend was.

Merovech was the son of the queen, Chlodio's wife; but his father was a sea-god, *bistea Neptuni* . Perhaps you may think that the existence of this legend is sufficient to throw doubt on the very existence of Merovech. That would be a hasty conclusion. The fact that Merovech comes in between the historical Chlodio and the historical Childeric seems to be a certain guarantee of his reality. If he were merely, as has been supposed, the legendary founder of the Merovingian family, then legend would have placed him before, not after, Chlodio. The legend is probably simply an attempt to explain his name, which means Son of the Sea.

Childeric is a somewhat clearer figure than Chlodio, but around him too legends grew up in which popular imagination dealt freely with historical facts. These legends were known to Gregory of Tours and Fredegarius, and they have preserved not very much, but at least some indications which are of service. There was a tale which told how Childeric and his mother were led into captivity by the Huns, and how he was delivered by the loyalty and devotion of a Frank, Wiomad, who enabled him to escape. This was a common type of tale – we have other examples – escape from captivity achieved through the cunning of a faithful and crafty esquire or servant. But you observe that the historical setting is accurate; it is perfectly in accordance with probability that Childeric, then a youth, might have been captured when Attila invaded Gaul. In my opinion, so much of the story is probably true: an actual captivity of Childeric at the Hunnic court is the most likely explanation of the origin of the story, which must have had a historical motif. And if so, it will follow that it was not Childeric, but his father, Merovech, who was present at the Mauriac battle.

The other legend of Childeric to which I must refer is that of his marriage. The name of his wife was Basina; she was the mother of the great Clovis. As to her reality there can, I think, be no doubt. The name of Clovis's mother must have been remembered, and besides we know that at a later time Basina was a name in the Merovingian family. But a curious story was set afloat as to who Basina was and how Childeric came to marry her. It was related that Childeric led such a dissolute life, and committed so many acts of violence, that the Franks were roused to indignation against him and he was forced to flee. Before he fled, one of his friends, the faithful Wiomad, undertook to appease the people during his absence and prepare the way for his return. They split a piece of gold, and Wiomad was to send his half to Childeric as a token when the favourable time had come. Childeric found refuge in Thuringia with King Basinus and his wife Basina. The Franks then chose the Roman general Aegidius as their king. Through the machinations of Wiomad, the rule of Aegidius became heavy and unpopular, so that at the end of eight years the Franks regretted their exiled monarch. Wiomad then sent the token; Childeric returned to his land and resumed his kingship. Shortly afterwards Basina left her husband and fled to the homestead of Childeric. When he asked her why she had come so far, she replied, "Because I know your bravery. If I had thought that there was one braver than you, even beyond the sea, I would have sought him." Then Childeric took her to wife.

I need hardly point out to you the legendary shape of this narrative, whatever facts underlie it. It can be shown that two distinct legends and motifs have been combined. You observe the incongruity of the dialogue between Childeric and Basina with what goes before. Childeric has been living for eight years at her court, and yet he asks her why she has come, as if he had not the faintest suspicion. The dialogue, in fact, presumes no previous acquaintance. This suggests that originally the story of Childeric's meeting with Basina had no connection with the story of his exile in Thuringia. The combination of the two stories was a later thought. And of course it is an absurdity, or at the best highly improbable, to suppose that Basina was the wife of Basinus the Thuringian king. Basinus and Basina ought to be the names of brother and sister, but it was not likely to happen that they should be the names of king and queen. Basinus, or rather Bisinus, king of Thuringia, was a historical person; we have indisputable evidence of his existence; but Kurth is perhaps right in his view that it was just the resemblance of names between the historical Basina and the historical Basinus (each of whom came into a story about Childeric) that suggested the interlacing of the two stories. How much historical fact may we glean from these traditions? From the one, we can only infer that Basina was the name of

Childeric's wife and Clovis's mother. The original legend represented her as coming to the king of the Franks, somewhat like the Queen of Sheba to Solomon; but we do not know whence she came. The other tradition, which represents Childeric as exile in Thuringia and the Franks submitting to the sway of the Roman general Aegidius, has undoubtedly an historical motif, and I venture to think that we can disengage its main significance. Observe, to begin with, that the introduction of Aegidius is quite in harmony with the historical circumstances of Childeric's reign, for just as Chlodio's Roman antagonist was Aetius, so Childeric's Roman antagonist was Aegidius. The story that the Franks voluntarily elected Aegidius as their ruler can be nothing more than the legendary explanation of Roman success at their expense. If Aegidius drove back the limits of their encroachment, regained for the Empire territory which they had occupied, forced them to give tokens of submission to the imperial authority, such humiliation, puzzling to national pride, was presently explained in their poetical tradition by the flight of their king and their own free choice of the Roman conqueror. The main fact which we can determine is that in the days of Childeric there was, for a brief space, a rolling back of the Frankish advance, a revival of the imperial power in north-eastern Gaul. But it is certain that the legendary exile of Childeric to Thuringia must also have had a motive. Can we determine that too? I suggest that we can. If the Franks were decisively driven back by Aegidius, what did that mean but that the territory over which Chlodio had extended his power was recovered by the Empire, and the authority of Childeric was restricted to their old seats in the land north of the Carbonarian forest, the land which the Franks themselves, as we saw, knew as Thuringia. Here, I suggest, is the clue. The repulse of the Franks into the western, the Frankish Thuringia, from their more recently acquired territory, which passed from under their king's authority, was the motive of the story of their king's exile, and the double meaning of Thuringia was the circumstance which determined the character of the legend. The Childeric of history had to retreat into Thuringia, that was the historical starting-point of the legendary invention; only Thuringia as counted as the *eastern* Thuringia; and hence the retreat of Childeric was transformed into an exile at foreign court. For this exile a motive was found in the tyrannical government of the king; and it in turn furnished a motive for the choosing of Aegidius by the Franks as their ruler.

THE REIGN OF CHILDERIC THE FRANK

We must now turn to consider whether anything is known of Childeric's reign from sober historical sources, unmoulded and untinged by popular fancy. Gregory of Tours is our sole informant about Childeric, but fortunately he has derived some facts from the *Annals of Angers* to which I referred above. In the first place, we learn that Childeric fought at Orleans before the death of Aegidius. Now there is no doubt what this means. It means that Childeric and his Franks fought as the *federates* of the Romans in the great battle of Orleans, at which Aegidius defeated the Visigoths, in 463 or 464. As to this, I think all good authorities are agreed. And you see how this fact harmonises with the inference which we drew on the legendary tradition – namely, that Aegidius had reasserted imperial authority over the territory on which the Franks had encroached. The Franks are now under imperial influence.

The next operations in which we find Childeric engaged are also on the Loire, after the death of Aegidius, but still as a Roman ally, a Roman *federate* . This time it is not against the Visigoths that his aid is needed, but against another foe – a foe whom we do not associate with Gaul but with our own island. It is a notable fact that the Saxons in the fifth century attempted to found kingdoms in Gaul as well as in Britain; they sailed for the Loire as well as for the Thames. They failed in Gaul, but in other circumstances they might have succeeded, and there might have been a Gallic Saxony. It was a remarkable anticipation of what happened in the ninth century, when the Northmen did what the Saxons had tried to do and had only partly done. Yet the Saxons did leave a mark, though it was a small mark, in Gaul. Some of the settlements remained distinct until late times, especially in the Bessin, in the region of Bayeux. But in the time of Childeric they were a terror to the cities of the Loire. Soon after the battle of Orleans they seem to have plundered Angers (under a leader named Adovaerius – a name clearly the same as that of Odovacar, the ruler of Italy). On the death of Aegidius, which happened about this time, the defence of the Roman provinces in north Gaul devolved on a certain Count Paulus; and his task was to withstand the encroachments of the Visigoths and to defend the land against the Saxons. Childeric and his Franks helped Paulus as they had helped Aegidius, and fought against both Goth and Saxon. The first object was to prevent the Saxons from capturing Angers, and Childeric successfully held the city. This success was followed up by active operations against the Saxons, and finally Adovaerius was forced to submit and enter Roman service. The general fact then to remark is this: that the rise of a Saxon power in north Gaul was arrested at an early stage and frustrated by the united action of the imperial authority and Childeric.

After this, Syagrius, the son of Aegidius, is the representative of the Empire in Gaul, and we hear nothing as to the relations subsisting between him and Childeric. But we may consider it certain that there was no further territorial advance on the part of the Salian Franks so long as Childeric lived. Childeric died in 481, and he was buried at Tournai, which was his chief place. His tomb was discovered there in 1653, and in it were found the remains of his royal cloak, his arms, and many gold ornaments.

Lecture 13:
The Reign of Clovis

THE OVERTHROW OF SYAGRIUS – THE MARRIAGE OF CLOVIS AND CLOTILDA – THE CONQUEST OF THE ALAMANNI – THE CONVERSION OF CLOVIS – THE CONQUEST OF VISIGOTHIC GAUL – THE ABSORPTION OF THE RIPUARIAN FRANKS – RELATION OF CLOVIS TO THE ROMAN EMPIRE

THE OVERTHROW OF SYAGRIUS

In the last lecture I traced the first efforts of the Salian Franks to advance in north-eastern Gaul under their kings Chlodio and Childeric. Perhaps I should rather say indicated than traced, for the meagre notices of our sources amount to little more than an indication. We now come to the greatest of all the Merovingian kings, the creator of the Merovingian power, the man who stands out between Julius Caesar and Charles the Great as most powerfully moulding the destinies of Gaul. It is indeed only in the reflected light of what Clovis achieved that the small successes of his great-grandfather win their importance and significance.

Clovis, son of Childeric and Basina, succeeded his father in A.D. 481. Though darkness broods over his reign of thirty years, and though, considering the greatness of his work, we know little as to how he accomplished it, we have at all events some fixed chronological points for tracing his gradual advance. His first movement was against the imperial power which still maintained itself in a portion of northern Gaul, encompassed by barbarian kingdoms. Aegidius, the protector of Gaul, had been succeeded by Syagrius. We do not know what exactly was the official title under which Syagrius represented the Emperor in Gaul. Up to 480 the Emperor he represented was Julius Nepos, after 480 the Emperor whom he represented was Zeno; but Zeno at Constantinople could do nothing to help him. He was practically, though not formally, an independent ruler, and the Franks naturally came to regard the Roman province which Syagrius governed as his own kingdom. Hence he is called in their tradition "*king of the Romans*"; and what is more, he is looked upon as son and successor of Aegidius, who again is considered the son of Aetius. In fact, in Frankish tradition, the last three defenders of imperial Gaul appear as a dynasty of Roman kings, and a pedigree, mounting higher, was made out for them. That is a very interesting illustration of the form in which popular tradition expresses historical facts. Syagrius resided at Soissons, and against Soissons Clovis moved in 486. A battle was fought; it is generally called the battle of Soissons, though I do not think it was necessarily fought just at that city. Syagrius was utterly defeated, and he fled to the court of the Visigothic king at Toulouse. Alaric II., son of Euric, was that king. He was not prepared to go to war with the Franks, and when Clovis sent a message peremptorily demanding that he should deliver up the fugitive, he complied.

A famous incident occurred in connection with this conquest which is characteristic and instructive. There was found in the booty a beautiful vessel, a work of art, belonging to a certain bishop, and the bishop sent a particular entreaty to Clovis to restore it to him. Gregory does not mention the bishop's name, but it can be shown, almost to a certainty, that it was Remigius, bishop of Reims. The king desired to do this favour to the bishop, and he told him to come to Soissons where the spoils were to be divided. At the division of the spoils, the king requested his warriors to reserve this vessel for himself, and all consented except one, who declared that the king should not have more than his legal share, and followed up his protest by breaking the vessel with a stroke of his axe. The Frank was within his rights; the king was forced to suppress his wrath. But next year Clovis held a review of his army. Singling out the offender, he found fault with something in his equipment, and snatching a weapon from him threw it on the ground. The soldier bent down to take up the weapon, and Clovis split his skull with his axe, saying, "Thus didst thou to the vessel of Soissons." Probably this incident has an historical basis; it certainly is not a Frankish legend; it was rather derived from an ecclesiastical source, as the subject indicates; and it has been conjectured with much probability that Gregory's source was the *Life of St. Remigius*, the bishop concerned, for we know that this biography was consulted by Gregory. The instructive points in the incident are two: first, the policy of Clovis, though he was still a pagan, to conciliate the Gallo-Roman bishops; secondly, the limitation of the royal power at this period; the Frank warriors are all on an equality with the king at the division of the spoils; one of them fearlessly asserts this equality, and the king cannot resent it; he can only bide his time for revenge. Such an incident would hardly have happened a generation later. Now, in respect of this limited character of the kingly power, it is important to remark that there were other kings among the Salian Franks besides Clovis, though he was pre-eminent. There was a king called Ragnachar who reigned at Cambrai, and there was another, Chararic, both kinsmen of Clovis. It has been thought by some critics that these kings must have been suppressed, and all the Salians united under the sole authority of Clovis, before he conquered Syagrius and the Roman province. I believe that this criticism is wholly from the purpose. Gregory tells us, and his authority may very well be a notice in the *Annals of Angers*, that Ragnachar co-operated with Clovis in that expedition. and the tradition which records how Clovis marched against Chararic and destroyed him records this act just after the war against Syagrius, and accounts for it by the circumstance that Chararic held aloof from that war. The truth seems to be that it was his success in that war and the heightening of his prestige that enabled Clovis to take steps to make his own authority sole and undivided over the Salians, and to get rid of the other kings. As the stories of his dealings with these kings were derived by Gregory from native legends, and as legend could be taken for fact, Clovis's character would be established as that of a cruel and bloodthirsty tyrant. But an examination of them shows that no inference can reasonably be made; the means by which he is represented to have annexed the kingdoms of his kinsmen are certainly not historical; and national epics love a perfidious and successful hero.

There is, however, one chronological indication of Clovis's authority over the Salians. We learn that at this time, 486, he attacked the Thuringians. Now, an aggression against the kingdom of Thuringia beyond the Rhine seems at this period of Clovis's reign highly improbable, in fact out of the question; and therefore we may take it that the Thuringian name here too refers to the land of the Salians, the Belgic Thuringia, and that this expedition of Clovis was one of the steps by which he became sole sovereign of the Salians.

With the conquest of Syagrius the power of Clovis, as I have said, reached to the Seine. It was followed by a further extension, of which we have no direct historical record and which we can only infer from subsequent events, an extension to the Loire. Here the people with whom Clovis had to do were partly men of our own race – the Saxons, against whom his father and the imperial generals had fought together.

THE MARRIAGE OF CLOVIS AND CLOTILDA

It was probably in the early 'nineties that Clovis celebrated his marriage with a Christian princess, Clotilda of Burgundy, the niece of King Gundobad, the lawgiver of Burgundy. About a generation after this espousal, a legend grew up about it – a legend of which I must speak, because it has been taken for serious history and it has thrown a shadow over the character of Clotilda, and a still darker shadow over the character of King Gundobad. The story is told in the usual abridged way by Gregory; its details have been more fully preserved by Fredegarius. Gundobad, king of Burgundy, according to the narrative, killed his brother Chilperic, and flung Chilperic's wife into the water with a stone round her neck. Chilperic had two daughters, Chrona and Clotilda. Gundobad expelled them from his court, and they lived at Geneva, where the elder became a nun. Now as Clovis often sent embassies into Burgundy, he heard about the young princess Clotilda, and he despatched a trusty Roman named Aurelian to discover and have sight of her, if by any means he could do so. At Geneva he was charitably received by the two sisters. Clotilda performed the pious duty of washing the beggar's feet, and Aurelian was able to whisper to her and arrange a private meeting. He showed Clovis's ring and told her that Clovis wished her to share his throne. Clotilda said that they must ask her hand of King Gundobad, and urged great haste, fearing the return from an embassy of Aridius, Gundobad's chief minister. "If the ambassadors do not come at once, I fear that the sage Aridius will return from Constantinople and defeat our purpose." Aurelian hurried back to Clovis, who immediately sent an embassy to the king of the Burgundians. Gundobad did not dare to refuse the request of Clovis, and the envoys returned with Clotilda. They placed her and her treasure in a car, but she foresaw the arrival of the dreaded Aridius from Constantinople, and she said to the chief of the embassy, "If you wish me to reach your master, let me leave this car and set me on horseback; then let us ride with all speed. If I stay in the car, I shall never see the king". So they did, they left the car and the treasure behind, and reached the court of Clovis safely. They were barely in time. For Aridius had meanwhile landed at Marseilles, learned what was going on, and hurried to find Gundobad. "I have made a treaty of friendship with the Franks," said Gundobad, "by giving Clovis my niece". "That is no treaty of friendship," said Aridius, "but the seed of everlasting discord. Remember, my lord, that you killed Chilperic, Clotilda's father, drowned her mother, slew her two brothers. If she becomes powerful, she will avenge her kindred. Send an army in pursuit and overtake her". Such was the counsel of the wise Aridius, whose coming Clotilda had so greatly dreaded. Gundobad sent a host in pursuit, but it captured nothing save the car and the treasure. Clotilda, when she reached the frontier of Burgundy, had ordered her guides to devastate the country for twelve leagues round about, and when this was done she cried, "I thank thee, O God, for letting me begin my revenge for my parents and brethren".

The legendary character of the story is patent, but in this case the very basis of it is entirely fictitious. Clotilda had nothing to avenge; Gundobad had not committed the murders of which the story accuses him. His friendly relations with his brothers are, as it happens, attested in a letter which was written to him by Bishop St. Avitus to console him for a daughter's death. "On former occasions", says the saint, "you wept with unutterable emotion the loss of your brother, and your people sympathised in your grief". This passage does not refer to Godegrisil, another brother who strove with Gundobad and perished in the struggle; it must refer to Chilperic. The testimony seems definitely to exclude the hypothesis that Gundobad slew Chilperic, as the legend assumes. Besides this, the epitaph of Chilperic's wife, Clotilda's mother, has survived in a church at Lyons. Her name was Caretena, and she died in the year 506, many years after her daughter's marriage. This legend, then, of the wicked uncle is not in accordance with historical facts: how did it come to arise? It has been shown beyond question that it originated after the great war of A.D. 523 between the Burgundians and the Franks, in which King Sigismund of Burgundy and his family tragically perished. It was to explain the origin and reason of this later war, which seemed so tragic because the royal families of the two nations were so closely allied, that popular imagination invented the story. If Clotilda were not avenging some old wrong, how could she have permitted her sons to destroy her kinsmen? Thus was suggested the story of old wrongs, a former scene in a poetical drama of injury and revenge. The connection is manifested by the mode in which the crime is made in the legend to correspond to the revenge. King Sigismund and his wife were slain and thrown into a well; accordingly, Chilperic's wife must be slain along with him and thrown into the water; again, two sons of Sigismund perished with him; therefore two sons of Chilperic (who may have never existed) must perish with *him* . We can thus safely conclude that the true Gundobad was not the sanguinary tyrant of later tradition, nor was Clotilda the bearer of tragedy and doom to the Burgundian house as she appears in the story.

THE CONQUEST OF THE ALAMANNI

A war of far greater moment, a war decisive in the growth of the Merovingian dominion, broke out in the year A.D. 496. The kingdom of the Alamanni on the upper Rhine marched on its northern boundary with the territory of the Ripuarian Franks, and the Ripuarians had to suffer or resist Alamannic aggression. Thus we find the Ripuarian king Sigebert in a battle with this enemy, receiving a wound which lamed him for life. That battle was fought at Tolbiacum, now Zulpich, in the Duchy of Ülich, west of Bonn, which shows that the Alamanni had invaded Ripuarian territory. The existence of such hostilities could easily furnish the Salian king with a pretext for attacking the Alamanni, and he may well have posed as a protector of the Ripuarians. But his determination to attack them was a resolve of the highest consequence for the historical role of the Franks. It decided that their power was to be not only Gallic but Germanic. The conquest of 486 had been the great step leading to advance to the west; the conquest of 496 was the great step leading to advance to the east. The Frank power was to bestride the Rhine, and to lay the foundations of modern Germany as well as of modern France. In historical books, up to very recent times, you will find it stated that the battle in which Clovis overthrew the Alamannic power was fought at Tolbiacum. That is a serious error, and has no shadow of authority. There was, as I just mentioned, a fight at Tolbiacum, and it was a fight between the Alamanni and a Frank king, but the Frank king was Sigebert the Ripuarian, not Clovis the Salian. The great victory of Clovis was probably won in Alamannic territory; but we must not build on the untrustworthy *Life of St. Vedastus* , where, though no definite locality is given, it seems implied that the war was waged in Alsace.

THE CONVERSION OF CLOVIS

Not long after the conquest of the Alamanni an event happened of still greater moment, viz. Clovis's conversion to Christianity. Ecclesiastical tradition connected the two events, representing that Clovis had resolved to embrace his wife's religion in case he were victorious. There may indeed be a certain measure of truth in this tradition. We must, however, realise the circumstances of Clovis. Christianity had already made some progress among the Franks. His kinsman, the Salian king Chararic, seems to have been a Christian. Two of his sisters – one of whom married King Theodoric the Ostrogoth – were Christians, though of the Arian creed; another remained a pagan. His wife, Clotilda, was a Catholic, though her uncle, King Gundobad, was an Arian; possibly her father had been a Catholic. Thus in the king's own household there were warring faiths – a state of things which we so frequently find in the barbaric kingdoms – on the eve of the conversion of the king. A ruler of Clovis's intelligence could not have failed to discern the immense support he would derive from the Gallo-Roman Church by his conversion. His policy toward the Church, as illustrated by the incident of the vase of Soissons, indicates clearly that he was conscious of the importance of its support. But it was equally manifest that his Christianity would be worse than useless if it were Christianity of the Arian form. To embrace the Arian creed might have seemed the obvious course, seeing that his German neighbours – Visigoths, Ostrogoths, Burgundians – were all Arian. That would have been a fatal mistake; and we may be sure that it was neither an accident nor his own religious preferences, but his political perceptions, that helped him to avoid it. It would be absurd to suppose that he weighed in the balance of judgement the Arian against the Catholic doctrine, and decided on grounds of reason or theory in favour of the former. That is not the way barbarians are converted. On the other hand the influence of his wife Clotilda is supposed to have counted for much, and it might be argued that his choice of Catholicism was determined by the accident that Clotilda was not an Arian. I think we may safely impute much to Clotilda's influence in hastening Clovis's conversion – we have analogous cases in Kent and Lombardy – but I am inclined to doubt whether the existence of this influence was accidental. If we remember that the Burgundians were largely Arian, that King Gundobad was an Arian, and Clotilda was exceptionally a Catholic, it is certainly remarkable, if it were mere chance, that Clovis's choice should have fallen on one of the Catholic exceptions. I think I am not rash in suggesting that it was just because she was a Catholic that Clovis chose her out. If I am right in this conjecture the policy and conversion of Clovis appear in a new light. He still hesitated to become a Christian himself, but, appreciating the power of the Church, he saw what an enormous help it would be toward securing its confidence to have a Catholic wife; he saw of what use she could be in negotiations with the ecclesiastics. In this light his marriage to Clotilda has less bearing on Clovis's relations to Burgundy than on his relations to the Church. It was deliberately intended as a substitute for becoming a Christian himself, and it made clear what form of Christianity he would embrace, if he ever embraced any. But why did he hesitate? Here is the point where there comes in another influence, which has so often prevailed over statesmanship – the influence of superstition. Clovis had not the smallest doubt of the existence of the God of the Christians, but, believing in the existence of his own gods too, the question was, which was the more powerful? Could he safely abandon his own? It took him some years, and we need not wonder at it, to decide between two opinions, and perhaps to experiment. It was a question perhaps of testing the rival claims by what the rival claimants could do for him. It is related that the first-born son of Clotilda was baptised with the king's consent and then fell sick and died. Well, there was an experiment, and one which in the king's eyes must have seemed unfavourable to the claims of Clotilda's deity. It may well be that circumstances induced him to regard his victory over the Alamanni as secured with the help of the Christian God, and that this may have been, as tradition records, the final test which caused him to consummate his previous policy by joining the Catholic Church. Clovis was baptised, some think, in the church of St. Martin at Tours, in A.D. 496; he had recently taken that city from the Visigoths – a fact which has only recently been proved. The prevailing view, however, has been that he was baptised at Reims.

The incalculable importance of Clovis's adhesion to the Catholic faith has been fully recognised by historical writers. They emphasise it strongly as an event of ecumenical consequence – *Welthistorische Bedeutung*. What they have not seen clearly enough is that the event was not an accident or a sudden inspiration. It was, so far as I can see, the crown of a consistent, calculated policy, which displays Clovis's high intelligence and eminently statesmanlike perception. To suppose that he was not conscious of the political bearings of what he did, to believe that it was the toss of the dice or a freak of circumstance whether he became a Catholic or an Arian, is to hold an opinion of Clovis's mental power which is inconsistent with his great achievements. For observe that this was not a case of foreseeing future contingencies, or discerning the small germs of great developments; no second sight was necessary; it was simply a case of taking a wide and statesmanlike view of the political situation, estimating the conditions in which his kingdom was placed, and choosing the policy which would best tend to its consolidation. It was the sort of problem which has often occurred and has often been solved. But it is solved by reflection and craft, not by chance or the happy hits of an unthinking ruler. What makes us prone to misapprehend and misrepresent to ourselves the intellectual calibre of a statesman like Clovis is the circumstance that the barbarians, the Franks of Clovis's time, Clovis himself, had a naive side, and that this side – a certain simplicity and childishness, combined with cunning – is what is chiefly reflected in the traditions as recorded by Gregory of Tours and Fredegarius. And so an idea is shaped of a bold warrior, primitive and childlike in his notions, capable of astuteness and cunning in his dealings, but one with whom are associated no higher qualities of statesmanship, such as become the founder of a great state. Such a conception of Clovis cannot but be untrue; the paucity of our material unfortunately has suffered the error to exist.

I have given you the usually received account of Clovis's conversion, depending on the account of Gregory of Tours. It is, I think, in the main points correct, with the explanations which I have suggested. But I have still to tell you that a document exists which is, so far as it goes, of much higher authority than Gregory of Tours, and which creates a considerable difficulty. It is nothing less than a letter from Remigius, bishop of Reims, to Clovis himself; in fact, a political document of incontrovertible authority; but we must be sure that we understand it. Two letters of this Bishop Remigius to Clovis are extant; one of them, the less important, is an epistle of condolence on the death of the king's sister, Albofledis, who was a Christian, and from its tone one would certainly never suspect that the person to whom it is addressed was not a Christian. But the other letter to which I have to direct your attention suggests very strongly that Clovis was a Christian when it was written. The bishop exhorts him always to resort to the advice and counsels of his priests: *Sacerdotibus tuis debebis deferre, et ad eorum consilia semper recurrere*. He tells him: *hoc imprimis agendum ut Domini judicium a te non vacillet*. So long as there was nothing to determine the date of this letter, there was no difficulty, for it could be taken for granted that it was subsequent to 496 and Clovis's conversion. But it has recently been suggested that the letter contains an indication of its date. The bishop states his motive for writing to the king in his opening words. As they stand in the MSS. they are extremely obscure and indeed obviously corrupt. *Rumor ad nos magnum pervenit administrationem vos secundum bellice suscepisse. Rumor magnum* – I am not responsible for the gender, and I suspect neither was Remigius, but what the bishop meant was: "An important piece of tidings has reached us that you have undertaken the administration of" – something. *Secundum bellice* makes nonsense. The usual resort has been to insert *rei* after *bellice*, and the meaning is supposed to be "that you have undertaken for the second time the administration of military affairs". Such a statement is unintelligible in reference to Clovis. The words *secundum bellice* have been brilliantly emended by Bethmanns into *Secunde Belgice*, "that you have undertaken the administration of the Second Belgica". But if this simple correction is right, it would seem to follow, as Gundlach has pointed out, that the letter was dated soon after the victory of Soissons, which brought the province of Belgica Secunda under Clovis's power. That is, it would be written in 486 or 487, ten years before the date assigned by Gregory of Tours for Clovis's conversion. But the letter seems almost necessarily to imply that Clovis was a Christian when it was written. Therefore, concludes Gundlach, the story in Gregory of Tours which connects that conversion with the victory over the Alamanni is false. Clovis was a Christian before the battle of Soissons.

Now, if this view were true, we should be met by a considerable difficulty. Why should ecclesiastical tradition, which gloried in Clovis as the first Christian king of the Franks, have conceived the thought of injuring his reputation by representing him as a pagan during the first fifteen years of his reign, if he was in reality for all or most of that period a Christian? This seems to me a very grave difficulty, and I cannot help thinking that the general tenor of the ecclesiastical tradition must be correct. How then are we to interpret the letter? Are we to say that the tone of the letter and the expressions in it which seem to imply Clovis's Christianity are delusive, and that the bishop designedly adopted that tone with the purpose of suggesting that Clovis should no longer be content with showing goodwill toward Christianity, but should now adopt that religion himself? Foreseeing the probability of the king's ultimate conversion, the bishop might have taken upon himself, proleptically as it were, to address him as if he were a Christian. This is just conceivable, but I hardly think we could without distinct evidence admit it as a probable explanation.

Of course the simplest way out is to say that, after all, *Secunde Belgice* is only an emendation. But it is an emendation of a very high order of probability. The context requires the designation of a territory or province, and as the MSS. give *Secundum bellice* , it seems quite impossible to escape the conviction that *Secunde Belgice* is what the bishop wrote, seeing that the bishop's own see of Reims was in that province. We must admit, in my opinion, that Bishop Remigius in this letter did refer to the Second Belgica, but I am not prepared to accept Gundlach's conclusion as the only possible one. On the contrary, the evidence points, I think, to another conclusion of great interest and importance. Accepting the general truth of the ecclesiastical tradition that Clovis's conversion was not brought about till 496, it follows that this letter of Remigius in which the king's Christianity is implied was written after that year. Therefore it was after that year that Clovis undertook the administration of the Second Belgica.

It follows then that after the victory at or near Soissons in 486, Clovis did not immediately take into his own hand the direct administration of the provinces included in the so-called *regnum* of Syagrius; he left the administration to the imperial functionaries; he allowed the old organisation to remain unchanged; he contented himself with exerting a controlling influence.

Now, in the first place, this conclusion is probable in itself; it would show that the growth of the Frankish power under Clovis was more gradual than is generally supposed; not until after his great victory over the Alamanni did he feel in a position to exert direct and immediate rule over the Belgic province in which he had overthrown the regime of Syagrius, and to incorporate it fully in his dominion. In the second place, this conclusion seems to me more in harmony with the contents of the letter of Remigius. I find it very difficult to believe that that letter could have been written immediately after the victory of Soissons. It does not contain a syllable of reference to the battle, or to Syagrius. It is the letter of one who sympathises with Clovis, not of one who has just received the news of a very unwelcome fact of which he has to make the best. If it were really written just after the defeat of Syagrius, we should have to believe that the bishop was a traitor to the Roman government, and secretly favoured the Frankish invader: we should have to assume that the expression "You have undertaken the administration of Belgica Secunda" is a nicely calculated euphuism for "You have defeated our general".

THE CONQUEST OF VISIGOTHIC GAUL

Once the Franks and Visigoths came into close quarters on the Loire, war between them was inevitable. The decisive struggle was postponed for twenty years after the conquest of Syagrius, but the two kingdoms were never on good terms, and serious hostilities were not lacking. The Franks seem to have been always the aggressors. They were in possession of the city of Tours in A.D. 496. They seem to have seized the city of Santones (Saintes) and also the city of Bordeaux, before the end of the century. The policy of the great Theoderic, king of the Ostrogoths and lord of Italy, was to preserve peace among the barbarian kingdoms in the west. He was allied by marriage with Alaric, king of the Visigoths, and *probably* his authority was instrumental in deferring a Franco-Gothic war. The opposition between the two kingdoms was accentuated when Clovis embraced Christianity in its Catholic form, and when the time was ripe, he could profess to go forth as a champion of Catholic orthodoxy to drive the Arian heretics from Gaul. It was in the year 507 that he declared war and led his army south of the Loire. The enemies met not very far from Poictiers, in the *Campus Vocladensis* ; the Goths were routed, and their king, Alaric, fell; slain, it would appear, by the king of the Franks himself. Then Clovis sent his son Theodoric to subjugate all the land as far as the frontier of Burgundy. He himself seized Alaric's treasure at Toulouse, and transferred it to Bordeaux, where he spent the winter.

Such is the brief story of this most important event, so far as it can be reconstructed from the records of the annals. The lordship of Aquitaine hereby passed from the Goths to the Franks; it became part of Francia in a wide sense of the term; and the authority of Clovis extended to the Pyrenees. The Visigoths were not indeed entirely driven beyond the mountains. They continued to keep, and kept throughout the Merovingian period, the territory of Septimania, with the seaboard as far as the mouth of the Rhone. But their centre was now transferred to Spain. Thus, with the exception of Septimania, Burgundy, and Provence, and the Breton peninsula of Armorica in the north, all Gaul was now united under the king of the Franks.

The overthrow of the Visigoths made a deep impression on the Gallo-Roman Church, and the impression is preserved in the pages of Gregory of Tours, who adorns his account of the campaign with various miraculous incidents, of which the ecclesiastical origin is apparent. The Gallo-Roman Christians, such as Gregory of Tours himself, looked upon the war as religious, and as justified by religion; the Visigoths were Arians, and therefore war against them was righteous, however unprovoked. Gregory represents Clovis as invading their kingdom without any provocation. "It vexes me", said Clovis to his followers, "to see these Arians holding a part of Gaul. Let us attack them with God's aid, and, having conquered them, subjugate their land". We need not take this story literally, but it expresses an important historical fact, viz. that Clovis's Visigothic war stands out among his other wars as one in which he had the enthusiastic support, not merely of his own Franks, but of the Gallo-Roman Christians and the Church. Soon after his return from Aquitaine, Clovis founded at Paris the Church of the Holy Apostles, afterward the church of St. Geneviève. The tradition was that before he set out against Alaric, he made a vow to build the church if he should return victorious, and marked out the limits of the site by hurling his axe, according to the German custom of taking possession of a domain. We cannot determine, and it matters little, whether he did make such a vow; the important point is that the clergy of the Church, rightly or wrongly, connected its foundation with the victory over the Visigoths. This, like many other stories which circulated among the Gallic ecclesiastics, may have no historical actuality; but they have all collectively historical importance – we may say historical truth – in reflecting accurately the impression which the conquest of the Visigothic kingdom made upon Gaul and especially upon the Church.

The enlargement of his kingdom by the annexation of south-western Gaul altered the centre of the realm, and rendered it expedient for the king to move his residence farther west than Soissons. He fixed on Paris, which then, at the very moment when the greater part of Gaul became co-extensive with Francia, was chosen for preëminence – a preëminence soon lost amid the divisions of the kingdom, but finally reasserted in confirmation of Clovis's choice.

THE ABSORPTION OF THE RIPUARIAN FRANKS

The kingdom of the Ripuarian Franks, of which the centre was at Cöln, seems to have maintained its independence, or at least its separate existence, till after the Visigothic War. But at last it fell into Clovis's hand, and Clovis was elected king by the Ripuarian Franks. This seems to be the utmost one can say with certainty. Frankish legend described this political change as a tragic catastrophe. Sigebert, king of the Ripuarians, had a son named Chloderic, and Clovis secretly suggested to Chloderic to kill his old father and reign in his stead. Accordingly Sigebert was slain by his son, and then Clovis perfidiously slew the son and caused himself to be elected king. I am only summing up a story that is handed down with details which show its legendary character; it is quite insufficient evidence on which to condemn Clovis either of fraud or of violence in this matter. It may seem probable that Sigebert did die a violent death, but the true circumstances are unknown to us.

RELATION OF CLOVIS TO THE ROMAN EMPIRE

I have still to speak of Clovis's relation to the Roman Empire and the Roman Emperor. It is generally said that the advance of the Frankish power under Clovis is distinguished from the advance of the Teutonic power, such as the Visigothic and Burgundian, by the circumstance that there was no disguise about it; that, while those other Teutons were settling within the Empire, the Franks snatched provinces from the Empire and never professed to be inside it. Now there is a certain truth in this view: there is generally a difference between the process by which the Franks formed their kingdom in Gaul and the process by which the Visigoths and Burgundians formed theirs; but this difference has been exaggerated. In the first place, remember that the Salians, like the Visigoths and Burgundians, were originally settled as federate subjects in an imperial province, and remember that Childeric throughout his reign acted as a federate and supported the imperial administration. In the second place, if my interpretation of the letter of Remigius to Clovis is right, Clovis maintained and supported the Roman administration in Belgica for a considerable time after he had overthrown Syagrius, and his attitude must have been that of the king of a federate people, not of an outsider. But the most important point is that his Gallic kingdom, when it was an accomplished fact, was recognised by the Emperor Anastasius as nominally within and not outside the Empire This fact has been questioned. It depends on a passage of Gregory of Tours which has been largely discussed. At the end of his account of the Visigothic War and Clovis's arrival at the city of Tours, Gregory goes on to say: *Igitur ab Anastasio imperatore codicillos de consolato accepit... et ab die tanquam consul aut augustus est vocitatus* . That is: the Emperor Anastasius conferred the consulship on Clovis and henceforward he was styled *tanquam consul* . This statement has been rejected by some critics as a fable because the name of Clovis does not appear in the consular lists. This criticism misapprehends the meaning. Clovis is not made a *consul ordinarius* , one of the ordinary consuls of the year. He received an honorary or titular consulship, an honour that was often conferred. The technical title of such an honorary consul was *ex consule* , and this is what is meant by Gregory's expression *tanquam consul* . The word *codicilli* for the deed by which the Emperor conferred the titular consulship is technical. There is therefore no reason to question the truth of Gregory's statement, while we recognise his inaccuracy in introducing the title *augustus* , which Clovis undoubtedly never assumed.

The founder of the Frank monarchy died in 511, and for the last three years of his life he was by virtue of his consular title formally recognised by the Empire. That title was doubtless a recognition of his championship of orthodoxy against the Arian Visigoths. Actually it made no change in the situation; but it is significant as illustrative of the relation of the Empire to the Germans who were dismembering it.

Lecture 14:
The Lombard Invasion of Italy

THE ORIGIN OF THE LOMBARDS – CHANGES IN SOUTH GERMANY – THE LOMBARD MIGRATIONS – THE ADVENT OF THE AVARS – THE DESTRUCTION OF THE GEPIDAE – THE LOMBARD SETTLEMENTS IN ITALY – THE LOMBARD POLITY

THE ORIGIN OF THE LOMBARDS

The Roman Emperor Justinian [A.D. 527-565] had hardly resumed the administration of Italy in his own hands, the Roman citizens had scarcely got rid of the foreigners who had been established in their midst, when a new host of invaders descended into Italy, to establish a dominion of a very different kind from that of Odovacar and Theoderic. The people who now appear on the scene are the Langobardi, who during the past four centuries have been moving about in central Europe in a way which it is very difficult to trace. We meet them at an early stage of German history, bestriding the banks of the lower Elbe, in the reign of Augustus. They are one of the peoples who feel the might of that emperor's stepson Tiberius. In the second century, at the time of the great migratory movements in Germany, they leave their northern home, and move southwards towards the banks of the Danube. In the time of the Marcomanni War (under Marcus Aurelius) they try to enter Pannonia, but are repelled. From this time to the fifth century their name disappears entirely from our Roman records. But their own traditions professed to tell their history during this period. Those traditions are preserved in a document known as the *Origo gentis Langobardorum* , dating from the seventh century; and in our main authority for Lombard history, the *Historia Langobardorum* of Paul the Deacon, who wrote before the end of the eighth century. Many attempts have been made to disentangle the movements of the Langobardi from these traditions, but none of them seems very successful; and, while I do not despair that it may still be possible to determine the history which underlies those traditions, I think we must content ourselves for the present with saying that the Langobardi lived and moved in the regions north of the Danube for the three centuries after the reign of Marcus Aurelius; and that they were necessarily included in the Empire of Attila. After the destruction of the Rugian power by Odovacar (487), it is said that they occupied the Rugian land on the north bank of the Danube over against the province of Noricum; but about 505 they were subdued by the Heruls and forced to move into the *campi patentes* , which must mean some part of the low plains of Hungary (which the Hungarians call the Alföla); between the Danube and the Theiss. Here they were neighbours of the Gepids who had occupied Dacia and part of Pannonia; and here they lived tributary to the Heruls for three years, and then about 508 they rose in rebellion and in a great battle they broke utterly the power of the Heruls. This war is described by the Greek historian Procopius as well as by Paul the Deacon. The Heruli or Eruli (the name is not improbably the same as *jarl* or *earl*) are a people whose wanderings are no less perplexing than those of the Langobardi themselves. After the break up of the Hun Empire they moved in the same geographical area as the Langobardi, north of the middle Danube. The war with the Langobardi almost extirpated them; the small remnant that escaped were partly settled by the Emperor in Moesia, and partly received into the kingdom of the Gepids. During the next sixty years the chief factor in Langobardic history was antagonism to the Gepids, and it was this mutual hostility of these peoples which led Justinian to offer the Langobardi settlements in Noricum and western Pannonia, to be a counterpoise to the Gepids, who were continually harassing and encroaching on the imperial provinces south of the lower Danube. During this period the Langobardi appear as useful and sufficiently loyal federates of the empire, not only helping it against the Gepids but also sending auxiliaries to fight against the Ostrogoths in Italy.

CHANGES IN SOUTH GERMANY

I must pause to point out some changes which had taken place, in these critical years, in the *south German* lands – the lands of the upper Danube. We saw that the Alamanni, after their defeat by the Franks, had settled in Rhaetia and the land which came to be generally known as Swabia. Their eastern boundary was fixed as the river Lech, on the banks of which is the city of Augsburg.

Now the future of the lands east of the Lech, and southwards to the Brenner, was decided about the year 500. These lands were occupied then by the Marcomanni and Quadi, who had been the leading peoples in the great German war of Marcus Aurelius. Their home was in Bohemia. Bohemia was originally a Celtic land: the name Bohemia is Boio-heim, the home of the Boii, a Celtic people. This was the name given by its German neighbours; but about the time of the Christian era it became a German land, being occupied by the Marcomanni.

The German period of the history of Bohemia lasted for about five hundred years; then its German folk migrated, and it was occupied by Slavs.

When the Marcomanni and Quadi appeared in the regions of the river Inn and the upper Danube, they were designated by the people of those regions as Bojuvari or Bojovares, "people from the land of the Boii" in fact Bohemians. From this name of the German settlers, indicative of their old home, the land was called Bajovaria, Bavaria. This is the origin of Bavaria. You see how the name is curiously derived from the same Celtic people who gave their name to Bohemia.

We cannot say how the Langobardi were affected by this migration which resulted in the making of Bavaria. I must now point out an important change of another kind with which the Langobardi are connected. It was probably in the course of the fifth century that the German speech in south German lands underwent a change which produced what is known as High Dutch or High German. This change seems to have worked from Burgundy in the west to Bohemia in the east; later on it extended northwards. The chief characteristic of this linguistic change was the shifting of the consonants, known as the "second shifting". The "first shifting", which is emulated in Grimm's famous rule, had affected all the Germanic tongues; the "second shifting", formulated in the same rule, was confined to certain geographical limits, and the language, so modified, afterwards spread beyond those limits. It is in consequence of this shifting, which may have been going on about the year 500, that the Germans say *Gott, zehn* , and *thal* , where we say god, ten and dale. But whereas in the first ancient, prehistoric shifting *all* the explosive consonants had been affected alike, according to the same rules, the second historical lifting was only partial; some of the consonants escaped altogether.

It especially concerns us now that the Langobardi came under the influence of this change. Their language, as they spoke it in Italy, exhibits the consonantal shifting which is the characteristic mark of High German. This fact is very important, because it is one of the data which enable us to determine approximately the date of that shifting. It must have been prior to the migration of the Lombards into Italy, because the Lombard language must have been affected by it while they were still in contact with the geographical region when the change originated and was consummated. If the shifting did not begin till the end of the sixth century, till after the Lombards had departed for Italy, it is inconceivable that it could have affected their speech beyond the mountains.

THE LOMBARD MIGRATIONS

Let us now resume in a few words the meagre outline of Lombard history up to the eve of their invasion of Italy. Their earliest historical seats were close to the mouth of the Elbe, between the East Germans and the West Germans. There they were neighbours of the Angles and the Saxons, and the memory of this ancient Lombardy was preserved in the Middle Ages in the name of the Bardengau on the lower Elbe. Migrating southward in the second century, they lived and moved obscurely in the regions of Austria and Hungary for more than two hundred years till they were included in the Empire of the Huns. Living in the neighbourhood of High German peoples, their tongue underwent the change which produced the High German language. At last the Emperor Justinian admitted them into the provinces which they had in vain sought to enter nearly four hundred years before when the Emperor was Marcus Aurelius. They were now *federates* and subjects of the Empire.

THE ADVENT OF THE AVARS

Towards the close of the reign of the Emperor Justinian, a hundred years after the fall of the Huns, another Asiatic people, ethnologically akin to the Huns, resembling them in character and manners, arrived on the scene to take their place. These were the Avars. They were not destined to create as great an empire as that of Attila, but they formed a strong power in the Danube lands which played towards the Empire a similar part to that which the Huns had played, and were a very important factor in the political situation during the second half of the sixth century. We first hear of the Avars in the fifth century, when they still lived beyond the Volga. In the reign of Justinian they moved westward; conquered the Sabiri and various other peoples north of the Caucasus, gradually moved across the steppes of southern Russia, till they reached the Dnieper and then the Danube. But in the course of this movement they seem to have left a portion of their people in the region between the Caspian, the Black Sea, and the Caucasus. There is at the present day a people called Avars in Lesghistan. It is a remarkable fact that these Lesghian or Caucasian Avars have a number of names and words which are identical with the names used by the ancient Huns, and this is an argument for the otherwise probable view that the Avars were a people very closely related to the Huns.

The first embassy of the Avars to Constantinople was in the last years of Justinian. Their chief at this time was Baian – the Attila of the Avars. He was determined to push his power and conquest very much farther to the west. When he reached the Danube, his way was blocked by the imperial power to the south, and by the power of the Gepids in Dacia. But he pushed forward in the north, and perhaps extended his power over the Slavonic peoples who during the past centuries had been steadily pressing westward to the Elbe. Certain it is that about the year 562 an Avar host invaded Thuringia and was defeated by the Franks. The Gepids were the great obstacle to Baian's designs; they showed no signs of fleeing before the Avars as the Visigoths had fled before the Huns. But their days were numbered. They had on both sides foes who desired their destruction – the Avars on the east, the Langobardi on the west.

THE DESTRUCTION OF THE GEPIDAE

It was about the year of Justinian's death (565) that Alboin succeeded to the kingship of the Lombards. Alboin saw in the power of the Avars a means of crushing the Gepids. He proposed a compact to Baian. He said: "Let us join hands and destroy these Gepids who lie between your lands and mine. If we conquer them, you shall have their lands and half the spoils". This alliance sealed the fate of the Gepids. They were conquered in a great battle, of which the date is about 567, and politically annihilated. This was the end of another of the great East German peoples, who, though less famous than Goths and Vandals, had played a considerable part in the Danubian lands. A new period in the history of Dacia ensued. That country now passed into the hands of the Avars, who soon extended their power farther west.

The destruction of the Gepids seems to have been, on the part of the Lombard king, prompted by hatred and vindictiveness, not by policy. He slew Cunimund, the Gepid king, in the battle with his own hand; afterwards he took Rosamund, his daughter, to wife, and, according to a doubtful tale, fashioned her father's skull into a drinking cup to be used at solemn banquets. But no sooner had the extirpation of his hated neighbours been completed and his passion of vengeance satisfied than he determined to leave his home in Pannonia and seek a new home in Italy. He may perhaps have come to the conclusion that the Avars would not be more agreeable neighbours than the Gepids had been. He is said to have made the Avars the conditional inheritors of his Pannonian territory. He said: "If we Lombards conquer Italy, you shall have all our territory in Pannonia; but you must promise that, if we fail, you will restore it to us". However this may be, Pannonia, on the departure of the Lombards, was occupied by the Avars apparently without consulting the Emperor.

Our authorities tell us that the Lombards were always few in numbers, and this fact explains some circumstances in their history. When they decided to attempt the conquest of Italy, they did not go forth alone. They took to themselves partners and allies. Men of various races followed their standards, but their chief allies were Saxons – a host, it is said, of 20,000 Saxons with their wives and children. The historian calls the Saxons their old friends – referring to the fact that they had in ancient days lived in proximity on the lower Elbe. It would seem to be implied that they had maintained relations with one another in the intervening period. It may be observed that in law and custom there were many points of community between the Lombards and the Saxons. After the conquest of Italy, the Saxons wished to live in their portion of the conquered territory independently and according to their own laws. But the Lombards would not tolerate this arrangement. They insisted that their confederates should live subject to Lombard rule and Lombard laws. Rather than submit to abandoning the laws and customs of their fathers, the Saxons left Italy, returned north, and sought to settle in Swabia, where after a protracted struggle they were nearly extirpated by the Franks.

THE LOMBARD SETTLEMENTS IN ITALY

The first thing to be noticed about the Lombard conquest in Italy, which began in 568, is, of course, the fact that it was only partial. The Lombards never ruled the whole of Italy, like the Ostrogoths. They never held Rome or Naples; they never held Ravenna until just before the fall of their own kingdom. Italy, throughout the Lombard period, was divided between the Imperial and the Lombard powers. In the second place, the territories of the two powers were not compact and continuous; they were scattered through each other; the Imperial possessions were not confined to the south nor the Lombards to the north. The main outline of this distribution of the peninsula between the Empire and the invaders was decided almost immediately. Alboin entered Italy in 568 and died in 572; during these four years the Lombards occupied, roughly speaking, the north of Italy, including both inland Liguria and inland Venetia; in the centre they conquered Tuscany and a large territory along the Apennines which became known as the Duchy of Spoleto; in the south they won also a large territory which became the Duchy of Benevento. But in the north the sea-coast of Liguria remained imperial, and likewise the sea-coast of Venetia, including the island settlements, which were soon to grow into Venice. After the death of Alboin very little further extension of Lombard power was made until the reign of Agilulf at the beginning of the seventh century. His reign may be considered the second period of conquest; but his acquisitions were chiefly cities in the north, such as Padua and Mantua, which were within the lines of the Lombard realm, as marked out by Alboin. The third period of conquest comes forty years later, in the reign of Rothari, who won maritime Liguria. Some thirty or forty years later again – the date is not quite certain – a Duke of Benevento conquered Otranto and the heel of Italy. This is the general outline of the extension of Lombard territorial dominion. Imperial Italy consisted of: in the north-east, Venice and a district reaching from north of Ravenna to the south of Ancona; in the centre, the Ducatus or Duchy of Rome; in the south, the Duchy of Naples, the toe of the peninsula, and for a long time the heel. Ravenna continued to possess the importance which it had held under the later emperors and under the Ostrogoths; it was the seat of government of the exarch, the imperial governor who controlled imperial Italy, uniting military and civil powers. It is to be observed that the north-eastern territory, which may be called in a special sense the exarchate of Ravenna, is separated by the Apennines from the Duchy of Rome, and at this point the two Lombard duchies of Tuscany and Spoleto met. This circumstance marks a weak point in the Imperialists' position, but it was partly mitigated by the fact that they held the strong and important citadel of Perusia on this line, and it helped to link the two frontiers of their territory.

The failure of the Lombards to win the whole of Italy is in all probability to be attributed largely to the smallness of their numbers, to which I have already referred. But there is another very important consideration. The Lombards seem to have been born landlubbers, though they had once lived near the mouth of the Elbe. They never took to the sea; they never created even the most modest fleet. This put them at a hopeless disadvantage for attacking such towns as Rome and Ravenna. The Lombards could reduce a strong inland town like Ticinum by blockade. Alboin took Ticinum after a blockade of three years. Theoderic reduced Ravenna, when it was held by Odovacar, in three years, but he did it with the help of a fleet of cutters. If the Lombards had had the instinct and sense to make themselves even a small fleet, their successes might have been considerably greater. This defect explains the fact that they never made any conquest in the island of Sicily. I may observe here that since the fall of the Vandals, the sea-power of the Roman Empire held complete control over the western basin of the Mediterranean up to the beginning of the eighth century, when the Saracens began to dispute it.

THE LOMBARD POLITY

Having seen the limits of the Lombard conquest, we must now briefly examine their social and political system. In the first place, how did they deal with the Italian population, how did they deal with the proprietorship of the soil? These questions have been variously answered. I must emphasise the fact that the Lombards, though they were *federates* of the Emperor in Pannonia, nevertheless, when they invaded Italy, did so without any regard to the federal bond. They came as undisguised enemies; they made no pretence of forming settlements as *federati* . In this respect, they are strongly contrasted with the East German peoples: even the Vandals made a compact with the imperial government. We might then expect to find that the rule and administration of the Lombards would be similarly out of relation to Roman institutions, and this indeed is what we find in Lombard legislation. The Edict or law code of King Rothari, which was drawn up in the middle of the seventh century, is like the Salian law – and in contrast with the Visigothic and Burgundian law – thoroughly Germanic from beginning to end. But the question is: Was there a dual system? While the Lombard conquerors lived by the law as laid down in Rothari's lawbook, did the Roman subjects live by their own Roman law, as they had lived under the Ostrogothic regime, and as the Gallo-Romans lived under the government of the Merovingians? There is no doubt that this was partly the case so far as personal law was concerned: the evidence is meagre, but there are one or two passages in the laws which can hardly be otherwise explained. In Rothari's law code there is hardly a reference to Roman subjects, hardly an indication of any difference of nationality, no provision for mixed suits. The inference is that mixed suits would come before a Lombard court and be judged by Lombard law. Troya and others hold the view that all the Roman population was reduced by the conquerors to the condition of serfs, or *aldii* . There were three classes in Lombard society: freemen; *aldii* , or half-free, who were bound to the soil, and correspond to the *leti* among the Franks; and thirdly slaves. The theory in question holds that all the Roman freemen were reduced to the condition of *aldii* and included in the second class. This view sounds very improbable. The solution which I believe to be the right one has been given by Professor Vinogradov in a book which he published a good many years ago at St. Petersburg, but of which the results are still little known in western Europe. I will summarise them.

In the first place Alboin took no general measures respecting the treatment of the conquered population: he died before he had completed the work of conquest. His successor Cleph contented himself apparently with the drastic measure of slaying or driving from Italy many powerful men among the Romans. After his death there was an interregnum of ten years, during which power was in the hands of the dukes; and they found it necessary to organise the conquest. What they did is thus described by Paul: *Reliqui vero per hospites divisi ut tertiam partem suarum frugum Langobardis persolverent, tributarii efficiuntur* . "The rest of the Roman population are distributed among the Lombard *hospites* , and have to pay them a tribute one-third of the produce of their lands." In other words, the institution of *hospitalitas* is revived in its older form; the proprietors yield a third of their *produce* , they have not to give up a third of their *land* . When he comes to the end of the interregnum, the historian Paul again deals with the condition of the subject population in a short sentence which has been much discussed and variously explained. *Populi tamen adgravati per Langobardos hospites partiuntur* . There can, I think, be no doubt that this expresses in an abridged form the same fact which was stated in the previous passage. "The subject peoples are distributed among the Lombard *hospites* " – *i.e.* among the Lombards whom they have to maintain as guests. The simple meaning is that when the royal power was revived at the end of the interregnum, the same thing was done as had been arranged before by the dukes in the several duchies. In other words, the plan of dealing of the Roman proprietors, adopted by the dukes, is organised anew, systematically, throughout the kingdom.

These general measures affected all the Roman land proprietors directly. They themselves, not their lands, were divided among the Lombards, to whom they had give a certain part of the produce, which was regarded as a *tributum* . Thus they remained proprietors; but they were *tributarii*. They were not bound to the soil: this is proved by the position of the *tertiatores*, descendants of these proprietors in the Terra di Lavoro in the eighth century. Hence the view that the Roman possessors passed into the class of Lombard *aldii* or serfs cannot be correct. They must have belonged to the class of Lombard freemen. It is possible that, as Vinogradov suggests, they formed a class of freemen known as *homines pertinentes*, mentioned in some of the Lombard laws and distinguished from the *aldii*. While the Roman proprietors were included in the free class, their *coloni* or serfs would naturally be included in the Lombard serf class, the *aldii*, and the Roman slaves would pass into the same class as the Lombard slaves.

To sum up: the main principle of the Lombard system was uniformity of government; the same territorial laws and administration applied to the conquered as to the conquerors, and these territorial laws and administrative institutions were Lombard, not Roman. The Roman population (while their personal relations were regulated by Roman law) passed according to their various social classes into the corresponding classes of the Lombard society. There was, however, one important difference. The free Roman proprietors had to pay a tribute of a third their produce to those Lombards to whom they had been assigned, and as *tributarii* they were dependent. You see then that the condition of the Romans under Lombard rule, though it was not so bad as some investigators have held, was very much harder than in those German kingdoms which were federate states, or had commenced as federate states, the Ostrogothic, the Visigothic, and the Burgundian.

Were there then no Lombard landed proprietors in the Lombard kingdom? Was all the land in the hands of the Italian natives? No. In cases where the proprietors had been slain or banished – and there were many such cases – the estates passed into the hands of the dukes or the king. These rulers made grants to their followers to reward their services and secure their loyalty. The principle on which these grants were made was in the interests of those who received rather than of those who granted. They were grants in perpetuity; no limits of time were imposed. Hence every estate granted by a duke tended to exhaust his capital. Moreover no conditions were attached to the grants, which conferred full proprietary rights. In the course of time the Lombard rulers came to recognise the defects of this system. Accordingly we find King Liutprand in the eighth century granting lands on long leases. We also find him conceding the practical enjoyment of an estate without any legal agreement or prescription. Such an estate could be resumed at any moment unless the occupier could prove that his actual tenure exceeded sixty years. From its very nature this mode of tenure left few traces of its existence – for its basis and essence was the absence of legal documents.

In the next lecture I hope to deal with the character of the legislative administration of the Lombards.

Lecture 15:
The Lombard Law

THE ADMINISTRATIVE SYSTEM OF THE LOMBARDS – THE CODE OF ROTHARI – THE LAWS OF LIUTPRAND

THE ADMINISTRATIVE SYSTEM OF THE LOMBARDS

The Lombard kingdom, like the Ostrogothic, kingdom in Italy was governed by a common and uniform administration, and it was subject to a territorial law which applied to all subjects, Roman and Lombard alike; the great distinction being that in the case of the Ostrogoths the territorial law and the administrative institutions were Roman, in the case of the Lombards the territorial law and the administrative machinery were Lombard. The independence of the Lombards from Roman influence is manifested conspicuously in the fact that they had no general system of taxes on imports. The absence of direct taxation was a characteristic of the Lombard regime. There was no staff for collecting taxes, and our authorities give no indication of any administrative difficulties connected with taxation, no complaints, no laws, such as are frequent under both the imperial and the Ostrogothic rule.

THE CODE OF ROTHARI

The first law code of the Lombards, the Edict of Rothari, exhibits no sign of Roman influence. Issued in A.D. 643 – seventy-six years after the conquest of Italy – its general spirit and character seem to take us back into the forests of Germany. We have here largely the same laws and customs which must have regulated the Lombard folk when it dwelled by the banks of the Elbe, modified at one or two points by the fact that they had embraced the Christian faith. The document itself opens with *In nomine Domini*. "In the name of the Lord beginneth the Edict which the Lord Rothari, King of the race of the Lombards, hath renewed, in conjunction with the chief men who are his judges."

The preface of the Edict goes on to say: "How great has been, and is, our care and solicitude for the weal of our subjects, the tenor of the following Code shows. We have been especially affected by the constant oppression of the poor and by the excessive extortions from those who are known to have larger property, having discovered that they are exposed to violence. So considering the mercy of Almighty God, we have seen the necessity of issuing the present improved law, which corrects and renews former laws, adding what is necessary and cutting out what is superfluous. We have embraced in one volume all that is required for providing that each man may live quietly, according to law and justice, and defend himself and his borders".

The first sections of the Code are devoted to offences against the king's peace. They deal with conspiracy against the king's life, with harbouring brigands, with exciting soldiers to mutiny, with the case of an officer who deserts his soldiers in a battle: all these acts are punished with death. "If any man take counsel with the king concerning the death of another or kill a man by the king's authority, he shall not be held guilty, either he or his heirs; because since we believe the hearts of kings to be in the hand of God, it is not possible for a man to escape whom a king shall have ordered to be slain." This important law, strengthening the royal power, basing it on a sort of divine right, is of course not ancient, but due to the recent growth of the royal power in Italy. The Edict goes on to enumerate various cases of life-taking: all of which are made good by the payment of a *guidrigild*, which is the Lombard name for *weregild*. Further laws provide for cases of annoyance or obstruction on the king's highway. Then we meet the crime of *walapauz* – that is of the thief who stealthily clothes himself in the dress of another man or disguises his face or head for the purpose of committing a theft.

It was dangerous to be found in another man's courtyard at night. "If a free man be found there and do not give his hands to be tied, and if he be killed, no compensation shall be claimed by his kinsfolk. And if he give his hands to be tied and be bound, then let him pay on his own behalf 80 solidi: because it is not reasonable that a man should enter another's yard at night in silence or secretly; but if he has any proper business, let him shout before he enters." This law strikes us as remarkable because the fine is so heavy: 80 solidi means £48, a sum which represented of course a much higher value then. A slave found in the same situation paid only half the amount.

Cases of sacrilege in churches next claim the attention of the legislator: then he goes on to enumerate, in a long list, all sorts of bodily injuries, in which the compensations are carefully assessed to the supposed gravity of the damage. This is one of the most primitive parts of the Code. If a man knocks out his neighbour's front teeth, he has to pay twice as much as if he knocked out his grinders. If you wished to cut off somebody's finger or toe, it would have been well for you first to refer to Rothari's list of fines; for if you cut off a great toe or a second toe, you would have to pay about £3: 12s., whereas if you contented yourself with the third or fourth you would get off with £l: 16s.; and, if you only cut off a little toe, you would not have to pay more than 24 shillings. But, as a matter of fact, Rothari had introduced a change in this tariff. In old days, the compositions were not so high. Rothari raised them; in order, he says, "that the feud may be postponed after the payment of these compositions, and more may not be required, but let the cause be ended between the parties, and friendship remain". Such were the means which Rothari adopted to attempt to mitigate feuds and private war. The next matters considered are injuries done to *aldii* or serfs, to household slaves, and to rural slaves. In all these cases the composition was paid to the lord of the injured dependent; and it is interesting to observe that in the case of some serious wounds the offender has to pay not only the fixed composition, but also a compensation for the loss which the master sustained by the man's labour, and the doctor's fee (*mercedes medici*). The treatment of accidents in the felling of trees is interesting. If several men are felling a tree and if it falls upon a passer-by and kills or hurts him, the men have to pay the composition in equal proportion. But if it fall upon one of the tree-cutters themselves and kill him, then one portion is reckoned for the dead man, and the others pay the rest in equal proportion. Thus if there are three men and one is killed, he is supposed to bear himself one-third of the responsibility, and the two others are only liable for two-thirds of the composition, *i.e.* each pays one-third. There is special legislation for poisoning cases. A free man or free woman who mixes a cup of poison, but has not been able to administer it, is liable for a composition of 20 solidi. If the poison is administered but is not fatal, the culprit must pay half the compensation that would have been due if fatal consequences had ensued. If a slave administer the poison, he is to be put to death, his master to pay the composition in money, but minus the market value of the slave.

Passing from criminal law, we come to the law of inheritance. The general principle was that of equal division among sons. So long as there was legitimate male issue, the daughters inherited nothing. But the peculiar feature of the legislation is the provision made for male children born out of wedlock. If there was one legitimate son, and also illegitimate sons, then the legitimate son inherited two-thirds, and the illegitimate sons, irrespective of number, inherited one-third. If there were two legitimate sons, they inherited four-fifths, and the natural sons got one-fifth. If there were three legitimate sons, the natural sons got one-seventh and so forth. But suppose there were illegitimate sons, and the only legitimate child was a girl, then the inheritance was divided into three parts; the daughter got one part, the natural sons one, and the remaining third went to the next of kin.

No man could disinherit his son except for certain crimes of a heinous kind, nor could any man convey his property to another if he had a son to inherit it. The laws about the donation of property are interesting. They take us into the ancient popular assembly, or *thing* : for the gathering of the people, which the Saxons called *gemot* and the Franks *mallus* , was known to the Lombards, just as to the Norsemen, by the name *thing* . Every donation of property had to be made in the assembled *thing* , and the Lombards in Italy coined the hybrid Latin verb *thingare* to denote the act of making a donation. The donation itself was called *gaire-thinx* . *Gaire* means a spear and must refer to some solemn form, in which a spear was used, for this mode of transferring property. A law of Rothari says: "If any man wishes to transfer his property to another (*res suas alii thingare*) let him not do it secretly, but let him make the donation – *gaire-thinx* – in the presence of free men, that no difficulty may afterwards arise". It was only men who had no legitimate sons who could *thing* their property. If such a childless man then wished to leave his property away from his next of kin, to an outsider, his only plan under the Lombard law (as there was no such thing as testamentary disposition) was to convey it in the form of a donation or *gaire-thinx* , with the specific condition that it was not to be actually transferred till the day of his death. There was a special form provided for this case: the donor had to pronounce the obscure word *lidin laib* . But the worst of it was that by this donation made publicly in the *thing* he limited his own power over his property for the rest of his life. He was bound for the future to enjoy his property reasonably, not to waste it or to dissipate it. Only if, being childless at the time of the *thingatia* , he had sons afterwards, then the act of transfer became thereby null and void.

We next come to the laws about marriage. Rothari formulates a general statement respecting the position of women in the following law: "No free woman, living in our kingdom under the *lex Langobardorum* , shall live *selpmundia* , *i.e.* according to her own freewill: she must remain always under the power of men, and if of no one else, under the power of the king: Nor shall she have the power of transferring or granting any movable or immovable property without the consent of him in whose *mundium* or guardianship she is."

The principle here enounced was of course common to the ancient German peoples, but nowhere do we find it so clearly stated or its consequences so fully considered as in the Edict of Rothari. The system was of course a great advantage to the women, in days when the blood-feud was an accepted social institution; and if the *mund* or protector of a woman was responsible for her acts, it was only reasonable that he should also have a voice in the disposition of her property.

The marriage laws have largely to do with the money which changed hands on such occasions. There were three different sums involved – the *meet* , the *faderfio* , and the *morgincap* . The suitor purchased the bride from her father or guardian, and the price he promised to give was called the *meed* – or, for the Lombards made *d* into *t* , the *meet* ; in making this covenant, the suitor required the assistance of a friend who guaranteed that he would fulfil it. Then the father had to give the bride a dowry, which was called the *faderfio* – father's fee. Then, after the marriage, the husband gave the wife a large present known as the *morgengebe* or in Lombard the *morgincap* . The laws provide what is to happen to these different sums in all sorts of contingencies. The lawyer has then to consider the cases of unequal marriage, between free men and free women, and serfs, or slaves, and the social status of the offspring in such cases. The only unequal union which was strictly forbidden was that between a free woman and a slave. A slave who marries a free woman incurs death, and the kinsfolk of the woman have the right of killing or banishing her and seizing her property. If they do not take action, the king's officer is to take her to his court and she is to be put to work at the loom with the slave-girls. On the other hand, if a man chooses to marry one of his own slaves he may do so, but he must first enfranchise her.

This leads to the subject of the manumission of slaves, and we learn of a very interesting process which must be Old Germanic. Let us take the case I have just referred to. A man decides to marry a female slave, and must therefore make her a free woman: how is he to set about it? He must take her to the Assembly and there he must transfer her by a donation, or *gaire-thinx* , to some other free man. *He* in turn must transfer her to another, and that other to a fourth, by the same process. The fourth owner will then lead her to a place where four roads meet, and there in the presence of witnesses will give her an arrow, the sign of freedom, saying the words, "You may take whichever of these four roads you will, you have free power". This done, the slave will be *folkfree* , entirely out of her master's power. In connexion with this, the question might arise whether a *Roman* slave of a *Lombard* master, thus manumitted, would live as a free man according to Roman or according to Lombard personal law. This case is dealt with by Rothari, who lays down that all freed-men who have been emancipated by Lombard masters should live according to Lombard law. This text is one of the clearest proofs that the Roman personal law existed side by side with the Lombard.

The laws dealing with fugitive slaves have considerable importance for the history of the decline of slavery. All men were bound to hinder the slave who was trying to escape. If a ferryman rowed him across a stream, being aware of his servile condition, he was required, on detection, to join in the search for the fugitive, and if the fugitive were not found he had to pay the value of the slave and any property he might have stolen to the owner, and moreover a fine of 20 solidi into the king's court. If the slave sought refuge in a private house, the owner was justified in breaking into it, in consideration of his *furor in servum suum* . If anyone harboured the fugitive or gave him food or showed him the way, he was when detected bound to search for him, and if he failed to find him had to pay the value of the slave and compensation for any work that had suffered through the slave's flight. Anyone to whose house the slave came was bound to give notice to his owner within nine days. The Church could afford no protection to runaway slaves. If a slave fled to a church or the house of a bishop or priest, he must be surrendered; and if he were not surrendered on the third demand, the bishop or priest who harboured him was compelled not only to give him up, but to supply at his own expense another slave of the same value. But it is most significant of all, perhaps, that a similar law is specially directed against connivance of this kind on the part of royal officers. The general inference to be drawn from this series of stringent laws – from which I have selected only some – is that general public opinion in the Lombard kingdom sympathised with the slaves. The laws strike us as an attempt to maintain the ancient legal institution of slavery, which is threatened by a modification or revolution in the feelings of the people at large. It is significant that the ferryman has to pay, besides compensation, a fine into the king's court. This suggests the interest of the king and the state in maintaining the institution.

The method of Lombard litigation is thoroughly Germanic. When a dispute arose between two free men, there were two recognised ways of deciding it, viz. the very ancient method by wager of battle which still survived, and the peaceable method of the oath, which is called in the Lombard Code the *sacramentum* . The mode of legal procedure was as follows. The plaintiff asked the defendant to give security for his claim, if it could be made good. The defendant gave a pledge, and also found a friend to act as a surety. Twelve nights were then allowed him within which to appear and repudiate the claim by oath. If illness or any other impediment occurred, twelve more nights were allowed. He might go on alleging excuses and postponing for a whole year, but at the end of a year, judgement would be made against him by default. The plaintiff on his part had within twelve days to choose six men from among the kindred of the defendant; but he must not choose any man who was known to be an enemy of the defendant. These seven, namely the defendant himself and his six kinsmen whom the plaintiff selected, chose five other free men, thus making twelve; and these twelve men were the oath-takers or *sacramentales* . They took an oath either on consecrated arms or on the Gospel – here Christianity introduces a modification of ancient forms – as to the rights of the case, and this oath was considered decisive.

This was the ordinary way of deciding disputes. But wager of battle, called *camfio* , still existed. The kings, however, tried to restrict it. It is enacted that such questions as the murder of a wife by her husband, the legitimacy of a son, the right to be guardian of a married woman are to be decided by the oath of *sacramentales* , because these matters are too important to be entrusted to one man's shield. But a man who calls a woman a witch or a vampire has to prove it by wager of battle. I may mention that there is an interesting law bearing on vampires, which shows Christian influence. "Let no man (it is enacted) take upon himself to slay another man's *aldia* (female serf) or maidservant, on the ground that she is a witch such as they call *masca* ; for Christian minds cannot believe or conceive it to be possible that a woman could eat a living man from inside him."

THE LAWS OF LIUTPRAND

The next great Lombard lawgiver after Rothari was King Liutprand in the eighth century. His laws were issued in successive years between 713 and 735, and are preserved in a collected form. Their great interest lies in the indications they give us of the advance which the Lombards had made in civilisation during the two intervening generations, a period of seventy years. In the first place it may be remarked that the Christian religion of the nation is more clearly and emphatically reflected in the laws of Liutprand than in the laws of Rothari. It is expressed in the king's own title *Liutprand excellentissimus Christianus Langobardorum rex* , and in his prologue, which is marked by scriptural quotations. In one ordinance he acknowledges the direct influence of the bishop of Rome: having forbidden marriage between first cousins with the extraordinarily heavy penalty of confiscation of property, he states that he does so on the injunction of the pope of the city of Rome "*qui in omni mundo caput ecclesiarum dei et sacerdotum est* ".

The stringent laws against soothsayers and idolaters – laws which may seem to us quite disproportionally severe – are doubtless also due to ecclesiastical influence. The unfortunate man who is foolish enough to consult a male or female soothsayer has to pay a fine of half his own *guidrigild* , *i.e.* , half the sum which would be due to his relatives in the event of his being slain. And if any governor or officer fails to discover and arrest soothsayers who are living in his district, he is liable to a fine of the same amount. When a soothsayer is arrested, he is to be sold as a slave.

Laws respecting homicide and murder are generally supposed to be a good test of a people's civilisation. In this matter, the laws of Liutprand show a remarkable advance on the Edict of Rothari in the direction of severity. According to the old laws, a murderer had only to pay the *guidrigild* to the kinsfolk of the victim. On that system a wealthy man might murder seventy-four men without seriously diminishing his fortune. Liutprand enacted that in the case of murder (as distinguished from homicide, accidental or in self-defence) the culprit should be punished by confiscation of his whole property. If his property exceeded the amount of the *guidrigild* of the murdered man, the *guidrigild* should be subtracted and paid to the kinsfolk; the rest should go to the king's treasury. If the property was less than the *guidrigild* , then the murderer should be handed over to the kinsfolk to be used as a slave.

Liutprand applied the system of *guidrigilds* in a new and quite artificial way. He fixed it as a penalty for a number of miscellaneous offences; such as when a scribe ignorant of law presumed to draw up a legal document; the crime of forgery; the giving to one man of a bride betrothed to another; or if a guardian consented to his ward's marriage in case she were a nun; or if a man married a woman whose husband was alive; in these and other cases the guilty person had to pay as a penalty the amount of his own *guidrigild* , whether to the king's court or to someone whom his offence had injured. You see that this is a completely artificial and unnatural system. There is no natural connexion between such offences and the sum at which the perpetrator's life was valued supposing he were slain. The justification of it in the eyes of the legislator was no doubt that it visited these offences more severely on members of the higher classes, who had higher *guidrigilds* .

The custom of wager of battle had not yet disappeared. We saw that in the Edict of Rothari there were some signs of distrust of this method of settling a suit. The distrust is greater, and is more emphatically uttered in Liutprand's laws. He says that evil-minded persons would sometimes challenge a man in order to vex him, and he considers cases where a man who was defeated in the battle is afterwards proved innocent of the charge. His attitude to the wager of battle is most clearly expressed in a law about the charge of poisoning. "Certain men have charged the relatives of a man who has died in his bed of poisoning him, and have, according to the old custom, challenged them to single combat. As the punishment of the murder of a free man is now, according to our law, the loss of the whole of the murderer's property, it seems to us a grave thing that a man should lose the whole of his property *sub uno scuto* through the weakness of one shield. We therefore provide that in such a case the accuser shall swear by the Gospels that he does not bring the charge in malice. On this condition he may proceed in his cause by battle. But if defeat shall befall him against whom the charge is made or his hired champion, then he is not to forfeit his whole property, but only to pay the appropriate composition according to the old law. For we are uncertain concerning the judgement of God, and we have heard of a man losing his suit by combat unjustly; but we cannot forbid the custom of combat, because it is an old custom of our Lombard race."

To show further how things were tending, it may be noticed that the position of women was improving, as shown by the law which gave a daughter the whole of her father's property when she had no legitimate brother, and by the enactments for protecting women against oppression and injuries from their *mandvalds* or guardians.

Also in regard to slaves, we find that a new and simpler method of manumission has been introduced, in addition to the old cumbrous process of repeated *thingations*. If the owner gives the slave into the hands of the king, and the king bids a priest take him round an altar, then the slave shall be free, just as if he had been made *folkfree* by the old process.

I may quote one curious case which came before King Liutprand, to illustrate what might happen in a Lombard village. "It has been brought to our notice", he says, "that some treacherous and malicious men, who would not venture themselves to enter with violence into a strange village or a strange house, through fear of having to pay the compositions which are imposed by the law, these men got together all the women over whom they had power, both slave and free, and sent them to a village to attack men who were a much weaker body. And the women attacking the men of that place beat them, inflicted violent injuries upon them with far more cruelty than men would have used. But when the matter was investigated, the men who were attacked had to answer for their violent resistance to the women. Accordingly we lay down that those men shall not have to pay any composition to the women or their male guardians, in case they have injured or killed any of them. Moreover, the public officer of the place shall arrest the women, and shave their heads, and distribute them among the neighbouring villages that in future women may not venture to commit such wickedness. And whatever injuries the women have inflicted on the men whom they assaulted, their husbands or guardians shall pay the legal composition. We have made this special judgement as to the punishment of the women and as to the composition, because we cannot bring the occurrence under the heading of an *arascild* or party fight, nor yet a sedition of peasants, because such things are done not by women but by men".

You may be interested by the following decision of Liutprand. "It has been reported to us that a certain man lent his mare to another man to draw a wagon, and the man had an untamed colt which followed its mother. As the man who borrowed it was driving through a village, some small children were standing in the street, and the colt kicked one of them with its heel and killed it. The parents of the child sued for compensation for its death, and the case was referred to us. Consulting with our judges, we gave judgement that the owner of the foal should pay two-thirds of the *guidrigild* of the infant, and that the man who borrowed the mare should pay one-third. We know of course that in the Edict of Rothari it is laid down: 'If a horse shall cause injury by its heel, his owner shall pay for the injury': but seeing that in this case the horse was borrowed, and the man who borrowed it was a reasonable being and might have called out to the child to mind itself and avoid the danger, we have decided that on account of this negligence he should pay the third part."

I do not know whether you will think that pure justice was done by this decision, but you may observe how the king acts here as a court of equity, modifying the operation of the law when justice seems to require it.

I may point out an important contrast between the state of the Lombards in Italy and the Anglo-Saxons in England. We find that the Lombard *people* had no influence in political affairs; the power of the popular assembly had entirely disappeared; but this is not all; the people had no influence even in local matters, and hardly any part in the administration of justice. The *thing* might assemble for the purely formal purpose of witnessing donations of property, but beyond such formalities no influence lay with the people. Justice was administered by the officers of the king. This is a very instructive fact, showing how far a German folk could travel from their old Germanic constitution, though they were not affected by the institutions of the Roman Empire, which in the case of the Franks and the Visigoths had a direct tendency in promoting centralisation, and diminishing the political rights of the people. It is contrasted, as I say, with the case of the German invaders of Britain, among whom local institutions were so important and so tenacious.

Printed in Dunstable, United Kingdom

64390474R00087